*My
Path of
Prayer*

My Path of Prayer

Edited by David Hanes

*Personal glimpses of the glory and the
majesty of God revealed through
experiences of prayer*

With a Foreword by Michael Green

CROSSWAY BOOKS
Eastbourne

First Published in 1981 by Henry E. Walter Ltd.
Reprinted 1983.
Revised and updated 1991.
© Crossway Books

ISBN 1 85684 019 0

Production and Printing in England for
CROSSWAY BOOKS
Glyndley Manor, Pevensey, Eastbourne, East Sussex BN24 5BS by
Nuprint Ltd, Station Road, Harpenden, Herts AL5 4SE.

Contents

Dedication and acknowledgements

Dedicated to all who are conscious of the inadequacy of their prayer life; to bring freshness to those who have grown weary of praying; encouragement to many who consider their prayer to be a feeble reflection of what it ought to be; and practical action for those ready to get into effective prayer in the power of the Holy Spirit.

My thanks and appreciation go to all the contributors, and to those who have encouraged and helped me in the preparation and editing of the book.

David Hanes

Foreword

I have only been sent three of these contributions to sample. But I can tell you one thing: I am longing to read the rest. These three give a wonderful flavour of what the rest of the book must be like.

First, they are utterly personal. You do not find here eleven famous preachers standing in their pulpits and thundering away on prayer. You find ordinary humble sinners (like you) wrestling away with it, and you feel a tremendous empathy with them.

Second, they are humble. They are indeed well-known Christians, but they do not give the impression that they have arrived. You find David Watson telling you he likes his meals too much to be a real professional at fasting, Richard Wurmbrand telling you how he forgot even the Lord's Prayer in the horror of continuous imprisonment, and Oswald Sanders confessing how his son's faith showed up his own lack of it in prayer. Such humility is both endearing and encouraging.

And thirdly, I love what I have read, because I find all the contributors really being practical in their prayer life. And I need that. I am not much good at praying: are you? I feel I need all the practical tips I can get. This book provides just that.

So I commend it as an unusually helpful contribution to the needs of ordinary battle-scarred Christians in the area of prayer, which is surely one of the most important, most neglected and most difficult aspects of our whole Christian lives.

12 August 1981   **Michael Green**

Preface

The basic truth about prayer is that God is even more ready to listen than we are to speak to him, and even more ready to give than we are to ask. Unanswerable proof is given in that verse 'he that spared not his own Son, but delivered him up for us all, how shall he not with him also freely give us all things' (Romans 8:32).

There are many ways of praying as this book reveals, but in the 'how' aspect of praying, we need to remember that the direction of our prayers is to Almighty God, who knows our inmost thoughts and desires. We do need to be taught how to pray, as a young child learns to talk or as adults we learn the technique of driving a car. Even the most natural actions have their technique, and a man has to learn to use even his most precious possessions. So it is with prayer.

As children we were taught to pray in a particular kind of way; for many, as the years went by, the habit of prayer was lost. Probably the reason that they had stopped, if they were really honest, was that they had not found prayer of any use. They possessed a very precious gift but they did not know how to use it.

In this book the reader will see how each author copes with the desire to have an effective life of prayer. For me it has been a moving experience to read and re-read the manuscripts; to let one's mind drift into each author's experiences. After reading a single contribution, you may well say 'I wish I could be like him', or even 'that will never happen to me', but our daily experiences of life are full of similar situations, and the examples in the book can be used as a guide. It seems wrong to try and be a shadow of any one of the writers—we have to be *ourselves*—but to learn from someone who has been 'through it' before us is exceedingly helpful.

As one is moved in the reading, the question we need to ask of ourselves constantly is 'what is God saying to me in this?'. Maybe a dramatic change in lifestyle to accommodate an hour of prayer and meditation daily, or perhaps just attaining new disciplines in writing down subject matters for prayer. A periodic self-examination of *how* we pray (time, attitude, place, subject matter, etc) is a revealing study, if we are really honest with ourselves.

Admitting *to God* the problems and failures in our praying would seem a good place to start, but God will not do for us that which we can do for ourselves. One thing is sure; a large percentage of ordinary Christians today have let their prayer times be squeezed out to second or third place as other demands have been allowed to have priority.

For one whose prayer life is so inadequate and in constant need of greater discipline and improvement, it has been a great privilege to be involved in the publishing of this book. I would echo David Watson's comments—'Certainly I have nothing to boast about, and much to confess with shame. I have anything but arrived.' Also, 'If some are encouraged by the truth that God's power shows up best in weak people (2 Corinthians 12:9) even in the business of prayer, this book will not be in vain.'

David Hanes

My Path of Prayer

Michael Baughen

*Michael Baughan went into accountancy and banking prior
to obtaining his B.D. at London University and his
ordination training at Oak Hill Theological College. He
served several parishes from 1956 to 1970 before being
appointed to All Souls, Langham Place, London. He was
Vicar 1970–75, and served as Rector from 1975–82, as well
as being one of the Prebendaries of St Paul's Cathedral. In
1982 he was appointed Bishop of Chester, where he has
been since. He is a frequent broadcaster and speaker.*

*He has a particular interest in Christian music for
congregational singing, which has involved him in editing
and composing for Youth Praise and Psalm Praise. He has
also written several books, including* The Prayer Principle
(Mowbrays).

*His wife, Myrtle, is a school teacher, and they have
three children.*

'Rejoice in the Lord always; again I will say, rejoice.' Paul was in no doubt about the priority of his life—it was the Lord himself. There is a marvellous buoyancy throughout his ministry and letters which stems from a man gladly submitted to the will and purpose of his Lord, whether it was in danger, suffering, persecution, joyful fellowship, evangelistic opportunity, in plenty or in want—in it all he rejoiced in the Lord. Prayer must begin right there. If we start with the idea of getting the Lord to do our bidding we are treating God like a genie of the lamp, on whom we call when we want our will done. Such prayer is an insult to God. When our life is put at his feet in worship and surrender then we want to do *his* will, and prayer is seeking to know and do that will. Prayer becomes the branch of the vine longing to do what the vine desires. Prayer is like the bride wanting to please her husband.

'Have no anxiety about anything' says Paul immediately after his words about rejoicing. How? 'By letting your requests be made known to God'—as simple as that! After all, he is in charge of his Church, he is the head of his body, he is the Lord of my life, so if I bring my requests to him I need not go on worrying about the outcome. He knows best. He has the power to do more than I ask or think. So I can have the peace that passes understanding. This takes all the huff and puff and straining out of prayer. Instead it is a marvellous relationship with the Lord—personally or as a church.

Of course, like any relationship, there are times when things seem outstanding and memorable. Sensing when the Lord is in an event or not is part of knowing him. I expect you could quote various examples of when you felt 'the Lord is in this'. Great moments aren't they? During my ministry in Manchester we all looked forward to the birth of a child to a couple. The husband's first wife had died of cancer within a year of their marriage. He had now married again, to a beloved Christian girl. Their first child was due. The staff team were all away at the Swanwick Conference Centre from Monday to Thursday. The child was born on the Monday and the news was telephoned to us that there was little hope—the child had been born 'cold' and was in an incubator. Immediately the staff team met in a room at Swanwick and prayed. The next day the news was the same—and the next. By now we began to sense during our praying that God was going to bring glory to himself out of this incident. On the way back home on the Thursday a quick call at the hospital confirmed that the baby was still in the same state. That evening was the church prayer meeting evening. Expectation grew that the Lord was keeping the child alive until the church prayed together. So it was. We gave ourselves in much love and carried this tiny baby to the Lord in prayer. The child responded AS WE PRAYED. Yes, we had sensed it right. The Lord was in that incident for his glory.

Small encouragements lead on to great celebration

Sometimes the Lord encourages us to see we are on track by a sign. Philip the evangelist had that encouragement when he ran alongside the Ethiopian minister's chariot—and he heard the minister reading from Isaiah 53. No need of further encouragement—Philip was on track! When I first began to feel my way in believing prayer regarding building projects, God encouraged me with such signs. We had the need to get a Curate's house and the perfect house came back on the market. We were short of the necessary money by £100—a lot in those days. We prayed. As we prayed the doorbell rang and a lady stood there. She said to my wife, 'I want the church to have my Defence Bonds—immediately.' They were for £105 but as they had not run the full length of time we lost £5. God's perfection in encouragement. As we began the actual building project of a new hall I wrote to the congregation suggesting that we thought in terms of gifts of £25 or £50 or £100. To many in those days it seemed a fortune. I had a visitor staying for a night. He picked up the letter. 'You don't honestly expect elderly people to give £25 do you?' The words were still on his lips as an envelope plopped through the letter-box. In it there were 25 £1 notes and a piece of paper signed by an old-age pensioner saying 'I wanted to be the first to give £25.' These were great signs of encouragement that we were on track and could go forward believing God was 'in this' and would see us through. Of course, such signs did not happen all the time—God gave them to encourage us in his love. As the years have gone by and I have been involved with projects running into hundreds of thousands of pounds I have seen the Lord 'in this' many times, seeing his people through to his glory. One such project was at St Thomas, Crookes, in Sheffield. They waited on the Lord concerning his will to enable them to have the buildings for his work. The bold plan was highly expensive to start with but escalated fearfully with raging inflation—moving from some £300,000 to £597,000! However much they gave, the target was still as far away due to inflation. It was my privilege to preach for them at the half-way point—a year before completion. If any body of people had cause for despair, they did! Yet they had been convinced of the Lord's leading, and were committed marvellously in prayer and giving to the hilt. There was much prayer for that Sunday evening. I felt that as I prepared the sermon on Malachi 3. I was absolutely sure that I had the Lord's word for them—I am seldom so assured. It proved to be a night of great significance—a watershed. The Lord met with his people and as the sermon was video-taped, all those not present shared in it over the next few weeks. During the next year the situation seemed more and more impossible—but the Lord is utterly faithful and on the opening day—just before Christmas 1980—the impossible was done. Given or promised: £598,000!! What a joy it was to share in the glorious celebration on that day and to preach a very different sermon from a year before! We cried and laughed together. Yes, his people had been right to sense that 'the Lord is in this' against impossible circumstances—and sensing his encouragement meant that they were drawn out in believing prayer and kept by his peace.

The assurance of the Lord's urging us on may also come as a corporate conviction. When we faced the challenge of rebuilding All Souls, Langham Place we faced a target of 3/4 of a million pounds. The conviction that the Lord brought to the Parochial Church Council became almost a burning flame in our hearts. We were not rash people. Yet humanly speaking we were foolish in the extreme to commit ourselves to such a gigantic project with only £26,000 in the bank. Yet, believe me, as we prayed and prayed and talked, we came to that conviction of heart that we could do no other but go ahead. It seemed 'good to the Holy Spirit and to us.' I have to admit to some cold sweat down my back but I knew that the Lord had given us this common mind and this incredible faith. Of course, he honoured it to the full as he always does when he is in something. After we began the rebuilding itself we had to face the question of whether the organ should be rebuilt at the same time. It needed it and it seemed the opportune time while the building was out of action—but did it not seem the piling up of the financial needs? We called a meeting of the whole church and in a spirit of prayer we talked about it together. It was one of those meetings when I did not have to take a vote. The Lord manifestly brought us to the conviction that we must do it. Little did we know that less than three weeks later a Christian lady in the USA would offer a gift for a specific item (the only gift like this in the entire project) and that the amount would be precisely that of the organ rebuild. We were left gasping with praise!!

Delays and doubts—for a purpose

There are also times when we know that the Lord must have an answer even though it seems delayed. We have peace that we are in his purpose and that what we are seeking is according to his will. We will do all we can to use our minds in seeking to act where possible but the answer does not appear—until the last minute. We have been praying for months regarding the need of housing in central London for an Australian family on our Training Course staff. To find adequate family accommodation near to All Souls and to the children's school in Victoria—at a price that was not utterly exorbitant—was well nigh impossible. Yet we were sure this was part of his will. The answer came a week ago as I write this, and with a week to spare. We had looked, we had advertised, we had prayed... and we had peace. Some answers to prayer are at the final moment. Bring your requests to him... and have peace, peace that passes understanding.

However, there are also times in prayer when we sense that

we are not 'on track'. Something seems to be wrong. The Lord does not seem to be in the venture even though we began in good faith. In Numbers 14 we have the incident after the spies returned from the promised land, most with an evil report and only Joshua and Caleb with a good report. The Lord judged the people for their faithlessness. They immediately responded by wanting to rush into the land, but Moses tells them 'the Lord will not be with you.' They are slaughtered. It might have been for them a 'faith-venture' but it was not the Lord leading them into it and the result—as has sadly often been repeated since—was the Lord's dishonour. So if we sense that the Lord is not in this venture, this prayer burden or request, it may be right to stop there and then and ask him where we have gone wrong. Conscious of our urgent need of a church hall close to the church in Manchester we began to pray. It seemed marvellous to us that in a short space of time a Baptist hall in the street across from our church was put up for sale. We gladly took this as from God and negotiations began. Then the Trustees of the hall could not be traced and there were all sorts of legal delays. We began to sense we were not on track. My churchwardens and I knelt down on the floor of the Rectory lounge and simply said 'Lord, what is wrong? Are we not acting according to your will?' When we stood up I was immediately seized with the realisation that we had never tested whether the scraggy piece of land behind the actual church was big enough for a hall. I took my wife's tape-measure and we went straight across to the piece of land. To our amazement it was just right!

In the next two days everything slotted into place. It all 'clicked'. We knew we were now on track and the hall stands there now as a witness to the rightness of its being actually attached to the church building and not across the road. Of course, as soon as we clicked to the new scheme the blockages to the old one were removed, but too late!

Having to learn lessons
Sometimes it is impatience that gets us on to the wrong track. Two years ago we came to the conviction that it was vital to

MICHAEL BAUGHEN

have an experienced lady worker on the staff at All Souls. We
wrote up a job description (as always, impossible to fulfil!) and
asked around. We prayed. We saw three possible ladies. They
were all splendid people but we did not have peace about any
of them. It was embarrassing but there it was. The Parochial
Church Council discussed it again. By this time one of our
missionaries was home on leave—Dr June Morgan. 'We need
someone like June Morgan' said a member of the P.C.C. Yes,
that is right. Slowly it dawned on me that it just might be June
Morgan herself. Dare I ask her? Dare I suggest her not going
back to Thailand? At an appropriate moment I ventured a
gentle remark. It met with a warm response. Then I learned
that June had the growing conviction that the Lord wanted her
to stay and be on the staff of All Souls and she was plucking up
courage to find the opportunity to mention it to me! God had it
all worked out. We had been 'off track' earlier because his
answer was not available at the time! We needed to wait for his
timing. How fully God has sealed June's ministry among us
since her joining the staff team.

We need to learn and relearn this lesson of not acting until
we know we have the Lord's plan. It is tempting sometimes to
be pushed into decisions and actions simply because action is
being demanded by others. I felt this deeply recently when we
were praying about a successor as warden of our Open Club-
house. I was bombarded with conflicting advice and pressured
to act. It was a painful experience to feel that even some of my
close friends were getting edgy about it. All suggested solutions were acceptable only to some. Then at the moment, when
I almost despaired, God gave the trigger I was seeking—
through the headmaster of our school—and the possibility of a
half-time teacher on the staff strength of the school. I could see
a way through. I tested it in several direction. The Lord sealed
it as his answer to *everyone!* it was God's answer—and was not
possibly a day earlier. Had we acted before that day we would
have been dreadfully wrong. Lord, give me patience to trust!

Another danger in prayer is deciding beforehand how God
should answer. We then look only in the direction from which
we expect the action to come and can miss entirely the way in

19

which God has planned to respond. We can also be utterly surprised about the way he works things out! In my early days in Manchester I was seeking to develop the ministry to students as part of the church's rôle in the area. I asked Dick Lucas to come up for an evangelistic guest service and asked him to preach primarily to students. There was not full support from the congregation—some welcomed the idea and others did not want students focussed on in this way. Yet the praying core felt this was definitely right. In the afternoon of the Sunday, Dick and I went out into the local park for a walk. It was foggy but not too bad. The afternoon was eerily still—not a movement of air. Then suddenly the fog came down like a blanket. It was hardly possible to see one's hand in front of one. My heart sank! Groping our way back to the Rectory we then had telephone call after telephone call saying 'we cannot come—impossible to be out tonight'. In the vestry Dick said 'Will there be anybody there?' We walked into the church. It was packed to the doors—with students! Only students and a few hardy folk from nearby braved that night and we suddenly realised how the Lord had sorted out the situation about ministering to students! He had answered our prayers in the most surprising way. The results in lives that night were marvellous. It also set the seal on the student side of our ministry from that day forward.

Sharing in God's purposes brings peace

One of the most sensitive areas of 'looking the wrong way' is over healing. It is the natural response of anybody who faces suffering in themselves or in others to look in every possible direction for relief or healing or deliverance. This can mean a loss of discernment about truth and even fine Christians have been tempted to turn to the most dubious 'healers' in their need. Yet this may be missing what God wants to do as we lay our requests before him. If we long most of all to do his will and to see his glory manifested, we will ask him to do what he deems best for his purposes. I have been deeply exercised recently by some specific cases of cancer suffering where the person concerned or a relative has believed that God *must* heal.

The theory that his kingdom came in Jesus and that all sickness can be conquered by prayer is attractive but does not square either with Scripture or with honestly-evaluated experience. The tragedy in the cases I have known is that God's glory is missed entirely during those years of failing health. Ministry to their soul is difficult because it is countered with 'I will be healed'. Witness to non-Christians is muted because instead of the glory of the Lord shining through in triumphant faith there is an almost frenetic pressure of prayer for a miracle up to the final day of life. Do I not believe God can heal? Of course I believe that and pray for it with faith—and have seen it gloriously happen. But there sometimes comes a point, as with Paul in 2 Corinthians 12, when after special times of prayer for healing God helps us to see that his glory is going to be through weakness and that his power is going to be shown through his grace in our frail bodies. More glory is going to come to him by the fact that we love him, trust him and adore him even in the midst of suffering and 'disaster' than by healing or deliverance. Once we have grasped that as *his way*, then it really can be a marvellous witness to him. The Christian's prayer must therefore be always for the Lord's will and that relieves all the tension. We put our requests to him, we share the problem with him, we leave this at his feet and we have his peace garrisoning our hearts and lives.

So, to me, prayer is a living conversation with my Lord. It is a fact of Christian living—just as sharing with my wife is a fact of marriage. I have found the value in recent years of a time each week in which I sit and think over things with him—things in the church, things in the family and in life itself. This comes after normal prayer and Bible meditation. It has been a delightful new dimension to my walk with him and in those times I have frequently grasped his vision and way. In the church we walk with him as the Commander-in-Chief. I am not the head of the work at All Souls—he is. That is a great comfort. We do not have to sweat at thinking up some new thing but rather, by meeting and praying together, seek to discern his way and then to get on with it in glad obedience. We are workers together with him. He leads. We follow.

The passage in Philippians 4 that I quoted at the start of this chapter goes on to speak of Paul's contentment: 'I have learned, in whatever state I am, to be content.' It is the testimony of a man to whom prayer was a vital but lovely sharing with his Lord and who, above all, wanted to honour Christ in his body—by life or by death. With Paul, let us 'rejoice in the Lord always'...and so learn how to pray, that the results will be evident as our hearts and minds are kept with the peace that passes understanding...in Christ Jesus.

My Path of Prayer

Derick Bingham

Converted through the work of C.S.S.M., Derick Bingham was a school teacher in Co. Armagh, N. Ireland, when called to be an evangelist in 1971. In the next six years he travelled to North America, South Korea, France and across the UK preaching the Word of God. He is presently with the Crescent Church, University Road, Belfast, in a Bible teaching ministry, and under God this has grown into a regular weekly Bible class which is one of the largest in Ireland. He frequently broadcasts on radio at home and overseas and is the author of several books. While at Queen's University, Belfast, he was awarded the university's Debating Society's 'Orator of the year' award for a speech declaring the Gospel.

I REMEMBER GAZING WITH wonder and tears of joy at my first daughter at her birth. It had been a long wait but there she lay, as Laurie Lee would put it, 'like a bruised plum'. I did not need to force myself into some corner and work up some great oration of prayer. My sinful heart, redeemed by the Lord Jesus, naturally and unforced, prayed God's blessing on her little head and welled up in a grateful prayer. I asked that her sinful but forgiven father would get the help he needed to bring the child up in the nurture and admonition of the Lord.

I remember such a prayer from my heart was edged by a question that seemed to crop up from nowhere on that August afternoon. The question was 'I wonder what I'll buy her for Christmas!!?'. Such a mixture brings, in my opinion, no dis-honour to the God who gave me that little bundle that day, all wrapped in white.

Prayer is for life and not for eternity. I shall not need to pray in Heaven. Since life is the environment of prayer, its multi-tude of circumstances deeply affect the way and the times I spend in prayer.

The supreme problem of the atheist is that when he wishes to be thankful, he has no one to thank. The supreme joy of the Christian is that, naturally, he immediately raises his heart to God in a grateful prayer when he has something to be thankful for. My way of prayer is to say 'thank you Lord' on the top of buses, in jet planes, when out riding my bicycle, when on the sidewalk, and even when gazing at a little white bundle in a hospital; anytime, anywhere, 'thank you prayers' are accept-able in his sight, my strength and my redeemer.

That prayer of gratitude for my little daughter was soon followed by a prayer of a very different kind. Four days later she took seriously ill. Like as though it were written in indel-ible ink on my memory, I recall opening a window with a breaking heart and looking up into the sky and asking that God would spare her life, but that his will would be done. That prayer brought me as much comfort as the prayer of gratitude. Throughout life my way of prayer is to send many such 'tele-gram' prayers to God's throne of mercy in emergencies.

My daughter was spared, but what if God had said 'No' to

that prayer? Would that have changed my attitude? I do not think so.

Recently news came of the death of a little girl. She had just had a major heart operation and the surgeon had said that of the several children who were having the same operation only seventy-five percent would survive.

When the news of the death of her child was broken to the Christian mother she spoke what I think were the bravest words possible—'He took our little girl because he knew we could bear it.' Such words do more for me than all the 'sermons' I have ever listened to. They touch something that is as deep as the promises of God.

Amy Carmichael put it very accurately when she wrote the poem about her own experience as a three-year-old—

> Just a lovely little child,
> Three years old.
> And a mother with a heart,
> All of gold.
> Often did that mother say,
>
> Jesus hears us when we pray,
> For he's never far away,
> And he always answers.
>
> Now that tiny little child
> Had brown eyes,
> And she wanted blue instead,
> Like blue skies,
> For her mother's eyes were blue,
> Like forget-me-nots, she knew
> All her mother said was true,
> Jesus always answered.
>
> So she prayed for two blue eyes,
> Said 'Good-night',
> Went to sleep in deep content,
> and delight,

Woke up early, climbed a chair,
By a mirror. Where, O where
Could the blue eyes be? not there;
Jesus hadn't answered.

Hadn't answered her at all;
Never more
Could she pray; her eyes were brown as before.
Did a little soft wind blow?
Came a whisper soft and low
Jesus answered. He said 'No';
Isn't NO an answer?

Nehemiah's 'telegram' prayer

'Telegram' prayers are frequent in my way of prayer but not
always when faced with extreme illness. I sometimes smile
when reading the story of Nehemiah because I can identify
with his need for a quick reply. 'What is it you want
Nehemiah?' asked the heathen King and Nehemiah says,
'Then I prayed to the God of Heaven and I answered the King,
"If it pleases the King...let him send me to the city in
Judah...may I have letters to the governors of Trans-Euphr-
ates...may I have a letter to Asaph, keeper of the king's forest,
so he will give me timber?"' (Nehemiah 2:4–8). If ever there
was a 'telegram' prayer it was Nehemiah's; it was sent silently
between two spoken sentences in a great eastern king's court
and it was answered just as quickly.

I often find in my way of prayer that not only do life's
circumstances affect my prayer life but the promises of God
undergird it. Recently the local BBC station called to ask if I
would be prepared to go on a discussion programme entitled
'What is an evangelical?' I was hesitant and the producer really
put the heat on, 'We have had a lot of letters and phone calls
asking us to put evangelicals on the air but we want to know
who they are. So many people claim to be evangelicals, please
would you try to clear the situation a little? Let's have your
point of view. It is a phone-in programme and people will ask
you questions.'

I said 'Yes' but with fear and apprehension! 'Lord,' I prayed in one of my 'telegram' prayers, 'What if the public eat me alive?! Anything can happen. Lord, I'm scared. I'm in no way able to take on this situation.' Indeed I was so nervous that the notion of 'crying off' was sweet to my taste until a promise from God came into my mind. 'When you are brought before synagogues, rulers and authorities, do not worry about how you will defend yourselves or what you will say, for the Holy Spirit will teach you at that time what you should say' (Luke 12:11). On the strength of that promise I went to the studios and found the promise was true to the letter. We should never be afraid of claiming God's promises both in prayer and in life because God loves us to believe what he says.

Prayer and guidance

In my experience I have found prayer to be a real key to divine guidance. I have found it vital to check three things when faced with a decision. First, is there anything in the Bible against what I am going to do? Second, what are the circumstances. Third, have I peace in my heart about it? If all three are one, I find I am on course.

Prayer always plays a major part in telling me whether I have peace in my heart or not regarding the decision about to be made. 'In everything,' writes Paul in Philippians 4, 'by prayer and petition, with thanksgiving, present your requests to God. And the peace of God, which transcends all understanding will guard your hearts and your minds in Christ Jesus.' In prayer that inner peace of God stands guard over my mind and heart guiding me what to reject or to accept. A non-Christian talks about 'gut feeling' but the Christian talks about the 'peace of God'.

In my way of prayer I have discovered that requests can be answered with unbelievable accuracy. Just like Jabez who cried out to the God of Israel, 'Oh that you would bless me and enlarge my territory! Let your hand be with me and keep me from harm so that I will be free from pain,' and God granted his request (1 Chronicles 4:10).

In my heart was a deep urge to write for children. Stories

illustrating the gospel, attractively presented, was what I was after. To produce these I obtained the help of an illustrator and with prayer in my heart I got to work on the writing. The printer got busy and the job was soon finished. His price was £250. I told the Lord about that too!!

The phone rang one afternoon. Could I come and meet a friend in Belfast? I left home and drove to see my friend.

'Is there any work for the Lord in which you are involved at the moment which needs some money?' he asked. It was an embarrassing question for Christian work is not begging. 'Come on,' he coaxed, 'my wife and I were praying today and God told us to approach you with some money. We had it set aside for his work.'

'I am producing some booklets on the gospel for children,' I said sheepishly.

'How much?' he enquired.

'£250 actually,' I replied.

Drawing an envelope from his pocket, and with tears in his eyes, he laid the little packet on the table.

'Inside you will find £250 exactly,' he said.

Expressing grief in prayer

Living and ministering God's word in Northern Ireland over the last ten years has taught me at least one thing, and I recommend it to all Christians. It is ALWAYS to pray with people in trouble if one has the opportunity. Grief must be given full expression if it is to be healed. There is no better way of expressing grief than by prayer.

I am not going to enter detailed descriptions of the political and religious divisions in Northern Ireland in this chapter; the world knows plenty about such already. All I want to say is that God has set a day of judgment in which he will judge every man by the one he has ordained to carry out his judgment, our Lord Jesus. On that day the correct view of everything and every deed will be given and the final judgment pronounced. Meanwhile sin abounds and where sin abounds, God's grace abounds much more, even in Northern Ireland.

Christians are not told that they will escape sorrow, even the sorrow of a church leader being murdered, shot in the back while in his grocery store. I rushed to his home on hearing the news and entered on grief such as I have never witnessed. I was disturbed almost beyond disturbance but somehow, not knowing what to say, I gently asked that we all pray. Everyone, including the police presence in that distraught drawing room got on their knees. Strangely, amidst tears, we discovered in a new way that prayer is a powerful thing and as Luther said, 'None can believe how powerful prayer is, and what it is able to effect, but those who have learned it by experience.' Out of that very house lives have emerged for the glory of God, amidst sorrow, which have warmed my heart with their witness to the unassailable truth that 'Nothing will be able to separate us from the love of God that is in Christ Jesus our Lord,' not even a terrorist's bullet.

At the Crescent Church in Belfast each Tuesday evening for nearly five years now, I am and have been faced with a congregation of hundreds of people, many of them young people, from every walk of Ulster life. They come for spiritual food, hungry and longing for a word from God's word. The counselling which follows these services has brought me to the position that I have come to look on every face as hiding a heart broken in some way or other. Yet I have found that to pray with each individual who comes for counselling has made all the difference. That includes prayer with people as widely diverse as a hunger-striker's prison nurse to a bride wanting to marry a chap with a terrorist ridden record! To pray with these people, to pour out their problems before the Lord has proved again and again the truth of Leonard Ravenhill's words, 'prayer is not an argument with God to persuade him to move things our way, but an exercise by which we are enabled by his Spirit to move ourselves his way.'

'I'm no C. H. Spurgeon!'

God's answers are, of course, thankfully wiser than our prayers. Through reading the life of Charles Hadden Spurgeon and what he accomplished for God as a young man I was deeply ashamed of my pathetic love for the Lord and my frequent and stubborn disobedience to his claims on my life. I was led, step by step by God's guidance to give my full time to the spread of God's word and the extension of his work, particularly amongst young folk. On the day I left school teaching a well meaning Christian just about broke my heart with trying to persuade me that I had just given up a position of great influence for the Lord to go,—what, preaching?!

I recall going to my home town that night and sitting down and crying my heart out. 'Lord, I'm no Spurgeon,' I prayed, 'but you called me and I ask you to use me for your glory. Although, Lord, I see no future in this position I'm in, humanly speaking, I'll trust you and go on.' No preacher ever started out as pathetically and falteringly as I did. I say this to encourage any young person considering giving all his time to specific Christian service. God has great surprises in store in the way he answers prayer!

Ten years later, after having been virtually around the world twice preaching the Word, I found myself travelling through London. I was on my way to make some Bible teaching broadcasts to be put out on radio stations in many different parts of the world. I could scarcely believe that God had led me, a sinful and disobedient sinner, first into his great salvation and then putting me in a place where I could speak to so many about the Lord Jesus. I was musing on this line of thought as the 'MG Midget' which had picked me up, wound its way from the airport to the studios. Then I noticed a sign on the road—it said 'Norwood'. 'But that's where Spurgeon lived,' I said to the surprised driver. 'Yes, indeed,' she replied. 'Could you take me to Norwood Cemetery where he is buried?' I asked. 'Yes,' she said, wondering what sort of strange Ulsterman she had on board!

I was soon standing where the great preacher and writer was buried and casting my mind back I remembered it was ten years since I had lain at home as a twenty-four-year-old reading of his exploits for God. God had not called me to be Spurgeon but the God who had called me was Spurgeon's God. How faithful God had been to me in answering that heartbroken prayer of mine ten years before. Bringing me to that graveside that day was just one of his personal reminders that he means what he promises. As William Gurnall put it, 'Some prayers have a longer voyage than others but they return with the richer lading at last so that the praying soul is a gainer by waiting for an answer.'

The best way to learn about praying is to pray. I go, sometimes, for 'praying walks', praying inwardly all the time I am out walking, pouring out my soul to the Lord. Sometimes I pray on the flat of my stomach on the study floor. Sometimes I kneel in prayer, sometimes I stand. Sometimes I shut my eyes in prayer, sometimes I don't. The Scriptures say nothing about keeping our eyes shut in prayer but they do talk about praying constantly and with faith. (Many people went to pray for rain during a certain drought, I'm told, but only one little lady turned up at the prayer meeting with an umbrella!!)

Prayer is conditional. If I cherish iniquity in my heart, the Lord will not hear me (Psalm 66:18). It is the prayer of a righteous man that avails much (James 5:16). I must constantly bring my sins under the power of the cleansing blood of Calvary (1 John 1:9) and seek God's glory alone in all my prayer life, then things will and do happen. If I find myself hating someone, I start praying for him and find him impossible to hate!

Prayer brings me to fix my eyes on the Lord Jesus and I have found that my feet always follow my eyes. I trust with God's help that my way of prayer will always be similar to my breathing, natural, unforced, regular and absolutely vital to my existence.

As prayer is only for life it is a very previous and short-lived privilege. Let us use it for the glory of God for I am assured by the little verse I saw etched on the gravestone of Charles H. Spurgeon,

'Then in an nobler sweeter song
I'll sing thy power to save
When this poor, lisping, stammering tongue,
Lies silent in the grave.'

My Path of Prayer

Jean Darnall

Jean Darnall, one of the few ordained women evangelists in Britain, is well known throughout most denominations here and abroad. American born, she lives in London where she assists her husband, Elmer, who is Principal of Christian Life College. Jean is author of Heaven here I come *and* Life in the overlap *(Marshalls). She is also well known as producer of three Christian musicals:* Come together, If my people *and* The Witness *(Word, UK).*

Prayer is my way to live. It is my pathway through life. Prayer gives to me a sense of direction. It is the upward way into eternal life.

My ways to pray are as varied as my life's experiences. My prayer moods are as changeable as an English sky.

The way I began to pray, to deeply pray with faith, has greatly influenced the way I pray today. It began in the church rather than in the home. My parents were not much good at praying until after their conversions, which occurred after mine. I was a teenager when an evangelist prayed for my healing of an incurable kidney disease. In answer to a very simple prayer of faith I was instantly healed. Such an expression of personal faith made me want to pray in the same way. Soon after my healing I sought and received saving faith from God and was able to confess my sins. Through that prayer I was born again.

Soon prayer opened my life to the fullness of the indwelling Holy Spirit. It wasn't long before I sensed God's call during a time of private prayer in my home. With daring faith I responded, 'Lord, I'll go anywhere with you. If you go with me, I'll go anywhere.'

As I waited, kneeling by my bed, the Holy Spirit brought to me a portion of scripture that became my very own promise.

'The Spirit of the Lord is upon me, because he has anointed me to preach good news to the poor. He has sent me to proclaim release to the captives and recovering of sight to the blind, to set at liberty those who are oppressed, to proclaim the acceptable year of the Lord' (Luke 4:18–19).

'Lord, that was your ministry,' I whispered. As I read the words he gave me another promise.

'As the Father has sent me, even so I send you' (John 20:21).

That experience gave me my first sense of direction of being led by the Holy Spirit. I was conscious of a clear course to follow. My soul was fixed on heaven. I knew what I wanted more than anything else in life.

'Oh Jesus,' I prayed, 'Here's my life. Add to it or take from it what you will, only there is just one thing I would ask, dear Lord. Please, when I have finished my life's work in your fields, let me meet you with my arms laden down with golden sheaves. Oh, don't let me meet you empty-handed. Give me, dear Lord, precious souls for my hire. When I reach heaven, however long that may take, give me the joy of bringing many others with me.'

That prayer has been the 'proof-prayer' of every other commitment, to line up all my goals with that ultimate one. I ask, 'Will this win souls? Will this have eternal value? Will this choice help me towards heaven? Is it upwards?' When I pray I am reminded of where I started and where I hope to finish. Sometimes I'm high in faith, sometimes low. Sometimes I'm moving along powerfully fast and at other times I'm painfully slow; but prayer keeps me going upward.

As I said before, my way of prayer began in my home church. My pastors were the ones who taught me its importance. Soon after I told them of my calling to serve the Lord, my pastor and his wife invited me to their home for a once-a-week time of prayer; not for dinner, not for talking, not for Bible study, but for prayer. I was enrolled in the school of prayer. I went directly to their humble parsonage from my high school each Wednesday. I usually found them on their knees. There was no eating. They fasted that day. At times they were bowed down in tears for their people. They claimed miracles by faith in the lives of those whose names they called out to the Lord. They wept for children, prevailed for whole families to be saved. In prayer they went up and down the streets of the neighbourhood asking for the souls of their neighbours. To my pastor and his wife those people were like lost sheep. Prayer was their way to them.

They believed as they prayed and with open Bibles they reminded God of his promises. They praised God for the answers before they came. When they asked for something they believed they had it. They were sure God wanted people to be saved, healed and to live victoriously. Arms upraised, shouting thanks to God. Other times they waited in long silences, listening. During those times I would almost be afraid to breath, the silence was so full of the presence of God.

After weeks of such rich tuition in pastoral praying, I was

allowed to stand with the elders in the church as they ministered to the people at the altar. I watched and prayed, observing how the pastor anointed the sick with oil. I listened as the elders prayed for some to be healed. Sometimes they would speak to the disease and tell it to go, as if speaking to another personality. I learned how to pray with those who sought salvation, leading them in their prayer of confession and acceptance of Jesus Christ as their Saviour. I saw the discernment and wisdom the pastor had and the elders in dealing with people whose problems were complicated, advising those who needed further counselling.

Then, one evening, my pastor asked me to anoint a woman who was sick and to pray for her. The elders laid hands on her along with me. I shall never forget my first thrill of actually ministering to the sick in my church. The local church was for me a house and a school of prayer. My pastor trained me to pray with spiritual authority. He taught me to prepare in prayer before ministry. Whether I was going to minister in church or visit a home or hospital, he instructed me to take certain steps in prayer first. I still use them before I go into any kind of ministry. Once in our vestry in Australia, before I entered the service with our guest speaker of the evening, I prayed in this manner:

'Lord, I thank you for the privilege of ministering to your people tonight. They are not our people, but yours. We are their servants for your sake. Cleanse us afresh by the merits of your shed blood. Forgive us of any sins which would hinder our relationship with you and our usefulness as a channel of your power. May Satan have no place in us. We commit this service to you. I bind the forces of darkness, every spirit of doubt or unbelief, who would dare to hinder the preaching of your Word and rob the people of the blessing you have for them. I bind evil forces in Jesus' name and forbid them to hurt or hinder anyone from receiving the gospel tonight. May the powers of hell be held at bay as we stand before you to minister. I also loosen the people to believe and to receive the gospel. We loosen those who have entered this service harassed and full of unbelief. By faith we claim them to be free by your Holy Spirit. We go into this service under the blood, relying upon the ministry of the Holy Spirit. Where the Spirit of the Lord is, there is liberty. Amen.'

I started to go into the church to begin the service. Our guest speaker, a missionary from India, stopped me. 'Where did you learn to pray like that? We need to pray like that in India,' he said.

Surprised, I paused and thought, 'Why, from my pastor, I suppose. He always prayed that way before he ministered and urged me to do the same. My pastor called it putting on the armour...preparing for victory.'

The missionary asked, 'Does a disturbance ever occur even after you pray that way?'

'Occasionally, but then I'm sure it is allowed since we've committed the whole service to God. I have confidence to act positively towards whatever occurs. Sometimes the disturbance reveals the need of ministry beyond the ordinary. When that happens, God always gets greater glory.'

During those early years my daily prayer life developed from simple morning and evening prayers into longer periods of intercession. My goal was to pray an hour. After praying the first day for all the missionaries and all their requests, I peeked at the clock to find that I'd prayed only seventeen minutes. So, thus, the ability to pray over longer periods of time grew and my ability grew to pray with the Holy Spirit and the scriptures.

My path of prayer is still influenced by those early experiences. I still believe God heals in answer to prayer. I can never forget how God answered prayer and healed my mother of a massive coronary and restored her to life. He healed my father whose lungs were ruined by chlorine gas during World War I. Later my husband and I prayed for our children. Our daughter was healed of congenital cataracts and eczema, our son of asthma. I tell of these and other healings in my book *Heaven Here I Come*. All of those experiences have greatly influenced our ministries and the lives of many others for whom we have prayed.

My path of prayer doesn't always produce instant answers. For instance, some healings were instant, others took years. The waiting time is the testing time. Prayer helps us to hold on to our faith while we wait.

One principle I learned early in our marriage has helped me ever since during the testing times. We lost our first child when we were missionaries in Panama. God spoke to me as I wept. It is the only time I would dare to say I heard an audible voice when he spoke. I heard him say, 'Faith doesn't ask why.' I wasn't able to immediately accept that word. When I did, it became part of my way of prayer and has helped to build a relationship of trust with my heavenly Father. To me, such trust is not mere fatalism, but an enduring faith.

Prayer is a very personal part of my life. That doesn't mean it is a hidden, private part of my life. I like to pray alone; indeed I must pray alone if I'm to maintain an honest relationship with God. I also like to pray with people. Whether alone or not, I like to pray aloud. Perhaps it is because I learned to pray with people who preferred to pray aloud with great fervour. In our church the whole church prayed all at once. Yet, it was not distracting nor confusing. There was an almost musical quality as they prayed in one accord. Harmonious. They prayed for people who had written in prayer requests. They prayed for one another about everything. Not just spiritual things, but about jobs, money, marriages, each other's kids and all kinds of troubles. They bore one another's burdens and joys. They had a shared life of prayer. Loving, practical acts of love would flow out of their prayers. The whole congregation loved to come forward to the altar to pray at the end of each service. On their knees, with arms around each other, more was done to heal hurts and reconstruct lives than hours of counselling could have ever done. I like that kind of praying.

Prayer to me is personal, not only by praying about personal needs, whether alone or with the church family, but because it allowed me to be more honest than in any other relationship. My moods affect my ways of praying. At times I'm articulate and feel my faith, my joy and can express it fluently. Other times, I'm hardly able to speak and feel nothing. Yet, whatever the mood, I know I'm accepted and loved. Such assurance motivates me towards prayer more than a sense of duty. I know it's right to pray and right to pray regularly. I know it is wrong to neglect prayer. Yet, the right or wrong does not make me pray; it is not the 'ought to' but the 'want to' that motivates me.

My moods make my prayers very much my own. I do not 'say my prayers.' There are a few prayers I quote. The Lord's prayer, of course, and some of the psalmists'. I love the prayer of St Francis of Assisi:

> 'Lord, make me an instrument of thy peace. Where there is hatred, let me sow love; where there is injury, pardon; where there is doubt, faith; where there is despair, hope; where there is darkness, light; where there is sadness, joy.
>
> O Divine Master, grant that I may not so much seek to be consoled, as to console; to be understood as to understand; to be loved as to love; for it is in giving that we receive; it is in pardoning that we are pardoned; and it is in dying that we are born to everlasting life.'

My prayers flow out of my heart's moods, my needs and are influenced by my surroundings and time. In the morning my husband and I pray. We begin by reading the Bible together. After we have thanked God for the day and other blessings, we pray for our children and our friends. We pray for each other and our work for the day. We do this in bed! Once our feet hit the floor, there seems more chance of prayer being rushed or omitted.

Every meal is received with thanks and a blessing asked. Even snacks are a cause of thanksgiving. I like to enjoy things with the Lord.

Prayer and praise punctuate my daily life...along with some groans and genuine complaints. I listen to songs and sermons on cassettes as I work. Often I join in by singing or saying 'Amen to that!'. Sometimes I pause and pray about some sudden reminder the Holy Spirit gives me about myself or another's need.

I like to pray with people who come to see me, either for counsel or a friendly visit. Sometimes I pray with them before we talk, always afterwards before they leave. Seldom does anyone leave our home without sharing our conversation with the Lord. Of course, if they've come for ministry, prayer is a vital essential. Prayers for people can be petition, blessing, healing, and deliverance.

After my husband leaves for his day at Christian Life College (where he meets with the staff for prayer before work starts) I usually have a time of waiting upon the Lord. I seek his counsel about our affairs, his will and purpose and ask for understanding of all the people I'll meet that day.

My path of prayer goes outside of my home as well as in it. One of my favourite ministries of prayer is while I sit behind taxi drivers as they drive across London. Often such silent prayers have helped me to open up a conversation about spiritual things. A few times I've had a chance to pray with the taxi driver before leaving him.

Often I am prompted to pray for strangers I pass or sit with on the underground or bus. Sometimes I suddenly realise the spirit of prayer is at work within me, even when I'm not aware of it.

My path of prayer also goes into other homes. I like to pray before I leave any house I've been in. I believe the Lord's instruction to his followers is appropriate today.

> 'As you enter the home, give it your greeting.
> If the home is deserving, let your peace rest on it;...
> (Matthew 10:13).

This also applies to towns as we enter them. We can bless them and also claim healing for those who give you hospitality (Luke 10:8–9). I have seen some fantastic answers right on the spot just before I have left a home. Sometimes more is accomplished by those doorstep prayers than by all the conversation during the visit.

Several years ago I recall asking a pastor to pray for me and for my husband and children as we went to minister in Australia. His abrupt reply startled me. 'No, I won't promise to pray for your ministry in Australia. I'll probably forget about you once you leave. I'm a very busy pastor. So, let's pray right now.' I thanked him for his honesty.

That experience has become part of my way of praying for people who are not my direct responsibility. When they ask me to pray for them, if at all practical, I stop and say, 'Let's pray right now.'

My path of prayer identifies me in different roles; a sinner asking for forgiveness, a growing saint waiting in meditation; a believer-priest in intercession; a spiritual soldier in spiritual warfare against the evil forces. To do these acts of prayer I may be kneeling, sitting or standing...or driving the car towards a place of ministry.

Prayer is necessarily a part of my decision-making. Right decisions within the will of God are impossible without prayer. Decisions usually come out of deep desire to do God's will. Discernment and faith follow once I begin to pray about God's will in a matter. Prayer moves my mind from my own fixed ideas of what I think God should do, to knowing and accepting what God wants to do.

In major decisions, once I sense God's will on a matter, I test it by asking for three witnesses to verify it. All three must be in agreement. I wait to act until they do. Without this confirmation, I act with caution and try not to make any further decisions about the matter until I see God's will more clearly.

The three witnesses are: a deep inner sense of God's will. The desire or urge to go a certain way or do a certain thing; second, a witness from scripture which I have not made a special effort to select, but which comes to me as a token; third, an independent witness through some incident which I have not influenced or through a person who knows nothing of my request. When all three of these agree, I act. Until they do, I accept that either my guidance is awry or my timing is wrong. I wait.

Let me emphasise, this method of prayer is reserved only for major decisions, not for ordinary, everyday decisions. God expects us to use our common sense and the knowledge of his Word and his will to make the day-to-day judgments. Daily prayer is usually quite enough to give us insight of God's pleasure or displeasure in most things. God should not have to give us so many confirmations as we mature and learn what pleases him.

My Path of Prayer

Edward England

For ten years Edward England was the Religious Publishing Director of Hodder and Stoughton. Today he is a publishing consultant and a literary agent for some of Britain's top Christian writers. He takes occasional courses for those who are beginners in the field and has himself written a dozen or so books. Since March 1981 he has been the Editor of Renewal *magazine, and also the Publisher of* Healing and Wholeness *since 1991. In 1984 he launched Highland Books. He and his wife Ann live in Crowborough.*

GWEN GAZED AT THE wide pebbled path which stretched from our sun-lounge alongside the fence to the foot of the garden. If she moved the pebbles she could make it into an herbaceous border with delphiniums, lupins, sweet williams, hollyhocks, red-hot pokers and Michaelmas daisies. It meant a few months of back-aching work and by the time the pebbles were all moved, and the soil was dug and mulched it was late autumn. The spades, forks, hoe and other tools were put away until the following Spring.

Gwen never saw the herbaceous border in full bloom. She died of cancer in March of the following year as the first of the flowers came into bloom.

For more than twenty years we had made gardens together. And for the same time we had prayed together, morning and evening. Now there was no-one to grow flowers with, no-one to pray with; the whole of life's rhythm had abruptly changed.

How does one pray when the eyes are filled with tears? I asked the question at night as I drew the curtains and kissed the pillow where her head should have been; and in the morning as I drew them back and saw the garden bursting into life. I no longer wanted to pray. Or to grow flowers. They were things we had done together.

In those dark days of loss, anxiety, self-pity, and unanswered questions, I made a discovery. *I didn't have to pray*. No preacher, no book, had ever told me that. God's love, his understanding, his companionship, were not dependent on my prayers. In this special circumstance I did not have to seek him—he was there. 'Talk to me again, when you're ready,' he seemed to say. 'I'll be waiting and listening.'

The realisation came as a relief. All my life I had thought I had to tell him of my concerns, to spell them out, to daily ask for protection for those I loved. In my grief I accepted that he knew, that there was no necessity to share verbally all the detail, that he came to me because I hurt rather than because of what I said.

His love was of greater consequence than my prayers. In a BBC broadcast one Sunday morning I heard the Methodist congregation sing, 'O love that will not let me go.' It came as a word from heaven. I wanted them to keep on singing. He who held the world in his hands, he who held Gwen in his keeping, he would not let me go. Not for a moment—and without my asking him.

They were days when I sought human voices more than God's. I kept the telephone by my side in the evening, and when the gloom deepened, I reached for it: to hear the buzzing sound, the receiver being lifted, a familiar voice—any voice— at the other end. Bereavement is like an illness. My healing began through listening each night to the music and songs of the Fisherfolk. They had presented me with some of their cassettes after we had published at Hodder and Stoughton their songbook *Sound of Living Waters*. The Fisherfolk had come to England from the Church of the Redeemer in Houston, Texas, and formed the Community of Celebration. Each night, before turning off the light by the bed, I listened to one side of their cassette. The joyful outpouring of praise and thanksgiving was a fresh experience. My heart lifted. Soon I knew the songs and began to sing with them: 'For you are my God'; 'Thank you, thank you, Jesus'; 'Blessed be the name'. Before long I was saying 'Good night, God,' before snuggling down beneath the blankets.

The unexpected death of a wife or husband throws all one's plans into confusion. The future one had dreamed of is no longer there. Priorities have to be reassessed. There is an urgent need for guidance both for the present and for the longer term. It has been the experience of Christians down the centuries that God does guide, that there can be a sensitivity to what he wants, that we do not have to stumble blindly. I copied out some words of Abraham Lincoln: 'I frequently see my way clear to a decision when I am conscious that I have not sufficient facts upon which to found it...I am satisfied that, when the Almighty wants me to do, or not to do, a particular thing, he finds a way of letting me know.'

That was my experience. I made mistakes. I started one journey into the wrong direction...and he showed me plainly in the six weeks that followed. I found peace only by making a humiliating and painful u-turn. Then that autumn I put up the house for sale. A prospective buyer appeared immediately. Later, he withdrew. I was disappointed. Now I see God was letting me know that this was no time to run from home and familiar things, that the year of bereavement was not the year for major decisions.

In my life I had reached a parking place. I didn't like it. A long journey from my twenties with Gwen, from saving a deposit to put down on a first house, through several job changes, had ended in my forties. Before another journey started there was good reason for reflection, a re-charge of the batteries.

'Learning to stop' said Michael Quoist, 'is the first step on the road back to sanity.'

———————

It was a twenty mile drive from my home near Tunbridge Wells in Kent, to the Hodder office outside Sevenoaks. It took about forty minutes, along winding country roads, past seventeenth century cottages, sometimes through historic Penshurst, with pastoral views as lovely in winter as any other season. For years I had switched on the radio as I took the car from the garage and listened to the *Today* programme, although I had already listened to the news while I shaved and had breakfast. I was a news addict.

One morning I found myself wanting to sing the songs I had learned from the Fisherfolk, music which represented God's praising people around the world. The tunes and the words had remained with me from the previous night. So instead of turning on my radio I used this journey as a period for worshipping God and saying my prayers. It was the start of a new pattern. Within a few days I had completely stopped turning on the car radio in the morning. The car became my sanctuary.

With the windows tightly closed, my voice so unmelodious, I sang 'Fear not, rejoice, and be glad!' Sometimes the glory of God filled the car. More than any friend, more than any book, this music ministered to me. My favourite song was 'We see the Lord'. Over and over I sang it. Instead of thinking of Gwen, instead of being filled with self-pity, I looked to see him, high and lifted up, and it gave a new perspective. In the dark I was seeing light.

Devotional writers have urged the need to find a quiet place for prayer, where we can be undisturbed: a room, a church, a garden seat. 'Our Lord explicitly teaches in his first great lesson on prayer,' says Dr P. B. Fitzwater, 'that the praying supplicant must above all else cultivate the habit of absolute aloneness with God in the closet or closed chamber of communion.' In this twentieth century, if there are no passengers, the car can be a closed chamber. I am often more alone in a car than anywhere. In country districts, and even in crowded London streets, it presents unique opportunities of absolute aloneness. Traffic with heaven in a car!

Into the passenger seat you may invite a special guest.

When Malcolm Muggeridge made his television film about the life of Christ he and a friend went on the walk to Emmaus like those two men in the Gospels who were joined by a third, a stranger, whom they later recognised as Jesus. 'We walked that road,' Muggeridge said, 'and I came to the conclusion that on the walk, or any other walk, there is this third man. He is there, he is available.'

There was now no-one to say goodbye to as I left home, no-one to wave to as I turned the corner, but on that morning ride through Kent, and on every drive, he was there, he was available. Once I made that discovery, to have silenced him by switching on the radio would have been rude. The news was depressing; the presenters obsessed with political and economic problems. 'When you see these things come to pass,' said Jesus, 'look up. Your redemption draweth nigh.' Looking up changed the outlook on the day.

Looking up I was reminded of a God before whom men cry, 'Holy, holy, holy, Lord God Almighty.' A holy God. A God of all might and power, creator of the earth and the heavens, of the sheep in the fields around, of the orchards, and the fields of ripening corn. 'O magnify the Lord with me,' said the Psalmist David. As A. W. Tozer has said he wasn't asking us to make God bigger. We can't do that. But rather that we see him big.

Prayer is not isolating ourselves from the world and so the world came into my prayers. I did not endeavour to mention everything, or all my friends, everyday, but there was a general pattern. There might be floods in the West Country or an earthquake in the Middle East. There were prayers for family, for colleagues, for authors. I talked with God about Tony and Jane expecting their first baby; about a secretary whose marriage was under strain; for a family of a colleague who had died of a heart attack on his way back from a funeral. He had been a scoutmaster, one of the fittest among us. I prayed for Richard, heading up our religious sales in Britain, and Helen selling Christian books in Australia.

I prayed about my own conduct in the office. 'Let your light so shine before men,' said Jesus, 'that they may see your good works, and glorify your Father which is in Heaven' (Matthew 5:16). 'Study to show yourself approved unto God, a workman that needeth not to be ashamed' Paul told Timothy (2 Timothy 2:15). My witness at the office was important; I spent sixty per cent of my waking hours there.

I had been impressed by an American book *The Christian Employee* by Robert Mattox which had been sent to me. The author listed seven precepts concerning our occupation. In summary, these were: God controls kingdoms and companies; we are employed by Christ, not by our company; our future depends upon God and our response to him; our circumstances are designed by God; our superiors should be counted worthy in thought, word and deed; we must trust the Lord to direct our career; our only status symbol must be the cross.

What a privilege! To start the day with God who controlled; to have this private conversation with Christ my employer; to be assured that he knew the timetable, the items that were in the diary, and the unforeseen events—the routine and the crises; to know that while my superiors must be treated with respect they did not direct my life. What a relief to find that if status symbols were given—the bigger office, the finer carpet, the better desk—that they were incidental. The cross was the Christian's only mark of prestige. There was constant pressure. Book jackets had to be initiated for forthcoming titles. Should we have full colour, or line drawings, or simply good lettering? A secretary wanted an extra fortnight's holiday to go to Canada. At 10 a.m. there was a management meeting; at 11.30 a.m. a publicity meeting. There was lunch with a Scandinavian publisher, an appointment in London at 4 p.m. Decisions, choices, non-stop for eight, ten hours. Estimates to be examined, printing orders to be signed, a telephone call to New York. It was fun, it was exhilarating, it was life. It needed prayer.

I shared with God about my authors. Writing demands isolation and some writers get depressed, losing faith in themselves and their work halfway through a manuscript. Sometimes I was prompted to send them a note of encouragement; an expression of the company's confidence in them; or on publication day a telegram of congratulation. Some, because of unexpected demands, had not been able to deliver their typescripts on time. Canon Michael Green, of Oxford, felt himself under attack as he gathered material for *I Believe in Satan's Downfall*. 'I don't think,' he wrote, 'that the Enemy wants me to write this book.'

Professor E. M. Blaiklock, author of some sixty books, living in Auckland, had lost his wife, Kathleen, after forty-nine years of marriage. His letter said: 'My family are wonderful, but after years of the most wonderful close companionship, I live on what so far seems unbroken anguish. The house in these lonely hills is crowded with memories—every drawer, every cupboard.' After years of ministering to others he needed solace. With prayer, distance was no problem. At sixty miles an hour along the Sevenoaks bypass I could remember him, knowing the promise of Jesus, 'Whatever you shall ask the Father in my name, he will give it you' (John 16:23).

Each day there was a fresh basket of letters waiting to be answered, another half-a-dozen book-length manuscripts on Christian themes, each submitted with hope and prayer.

'Make me sensitive to what they have written. In my response, Lord, make me conscious of the needs of the author, their disappointment if the book is rejected, their reaction if it has to be re-written.' Some manuscripts may represent the labour of years, or be the culmination of a lifetime's study, experience and research. 'Lord, we can only take a tiny proportion of what is offered. Give me wisdom, discernment, an alertness to what should be published regardless of economic considerations. Make me a good businessman. And make me more than just a businessman.'

We were given the privilege of publishing the *New International Version* of the Bible. It had been prepared by an international team of more than 100 scholars but the text needed anglicising for the British edition. How we needed heavenly support! Should our first printing be 75,000, 150,000, 200,000? The bigger the edition the lower the cost of each Bible. But if we had missed a printer's error—and we had only a few weeks in which to read the proofs—the smaller print run would have been better. Should we offer a variety of bindings and colours on publication day—or gradually build up a range? Should the service of thanksgiving be in St Paul's Cathedral, All Souls' Church, Langham Place, or at St Martin in the Fields?

On those morning drives I prayed more about the publishing of this Bible than about anything else in my career. It was a heavy responsibility. The investment for my company was considerable. More important, it was God's book.

By the time we had published the NIV Bible a new happiness had come to me. I had married Ann, a former missionary doctor with the Overseas Missionary Fellowship in Thailand. I told her about the Fisherfolk tapes but she had her own supply. In an isolated hospital at Manorom they had proved as inspiring as in my own solitude to me. In a land of spirit worship, they had known the same cascade of joyous praise, of awesome wonder, of sincerity and hope, which was accompanying the Holy Spirit's renewal in the church in Britain. We chose for our wedding service the song we had both learned to love: 'We see the Lord'.

Thanks to a generous gift we now have a cassette player in the car and are able to listen as we drive, not only to those tapes but to the expositions of God's word which are readily available on cassette. Long journeys seem shorter and less exhausting as we listen to distinguished preachers like David Pawson on the Epistle to the Ephesians. Today I have been listening to his introduction to that pearl of epistles. The car has become a place of instruction.

As a publisher I know that great writing often comes from great suffering, so I listen attentively as Mr Pawson explains how Paul wrote his letter chained to a guard from whom he could not escape, shut off from his friends. An active, out-of-doors man he was now enclosed, but from the irritating circumstances of that imprisonment came this epistle. 'It seems,' said the preacher, 'that the most precious things that God can say to people come to them when their earthly circumstances are very hard. When we go through rough and difficult times he speaks to us words that are more precious.'

I switch off the cassette and turn his meditation into my prayer. I recall those Christians who like the Apostle are in prison today for their faith; for those who are confined by illness or by caring for a relative who is sick. I pray that in their difficult times they may hear the precious things which he wants to whisper to them.

Through these tapes I learn that Scripture provides the perfect basis for prayer. The great promises of the Old Testament, the poetry of David, the prophetic chapters of Isaiah, the words of Jesus, bring into my heart a fresh dimension. I am no longer limited by the news. I am no longer confined by my own experience, my own desires, the selfish concerns of my life. I begin to catch glimpses of the glory and the majesty of God— the God of Abraham, and of Isaac and of Jacob, to know that their God is my God.

With David I confess my sin; that is the starting point for prayer—a cry to God for forgiveness; with Isaiah I hear the call of God to serve; with Peter I make the great confession: Jesus is God; with the Apostle Paul I name him Lord. I have published books of prayers but the Bible proves better than them all.

As I reach my destination, thankful for my safe arrival, I turn into the car park. Another journey over, another hour of spiritual renewal. Again I have found it possible to accept the invitation: 'Be still and know that I am God.'

My   Path   of   Prayer

Selwyn Hughes

*Selwyn Hughes is the founder and director of the 'Crusade
for World Revival', an organization primarily brought into
being to encourage Christians of all denominations to pray
for a spiritual revival throughout the world.*

He is the author of the Bible reading notes Every Day
with Jesus *and is involved in the teaching and training
seminars operated by C.W.R. in many different parts of the
world. A good deal of his time is spent in personal
counselling and he is responsible also for the training of
Christian counsellors in C.W.R.'s Institute in Christian
Counselling.*

*Selwyn Hughes is a Welshman, a widower and lives in
Surrey. He has two married sons and four grandchildren.*

MY PATH OF PRAYER has developed through a variety of different experiences and insights I have gained over the years, but *largely* through a dramatic event that took place some years after entering the Christian ministry. Ever since the days of my conversion in South Wales, in the year 1944, it was impressed upon me that a disciplined prayer life was the essential prerequisite to an effective Christian life. Later when I attended Bible College to study for the ministry I was told that there was no way to build a successful ministry which belittled, or ignored, or scamped the disciplined practice of prayer. The way to know Christ with intimacy, it was said, is to talk with him, to talk with him often and to talk for more than a few moments.

I failed to heed this advice. Oh, of course I *prayed*—I prayed for a few moments each morning, I prayed before meals, I prayed in the church prayer meetings, I prayed with people when I visited them in their homes, I prayed before I preached a sermon, but I lacked an organised and disciplined prayer pattern. I prayed only when it was necessary and failed to use prayer to develop and cultivate a personal relationship with God.

I threw myself into the work of the church with great enthusiasm. The result was I saw my church grow in numbers, increase its finances, develop its youth programme and outwardly I was regarded by my ministerial colleagues as a successful pastor. My church members complimented me on my enthusiasm, my preaching ability, and my organising skills but inwardly I was spiritually bankrupt. I felt like the man in the Old Testament who said, 'They made me a keeper of the vineyard but mine own vineyard have I not kept' (Song of Solomon 1:6).

Then just eight years after entering the ministry, came the dramatic event I spoke of earlier. I suffered a severe physical and emotional breakdown. It was so serious that the doctors warned my wife that unless they could bring down my temperature in the next three days it was unlikely that I could survive. Two days after they shared with her this alarming fact God miraculously healed me and restored me to health. It happened as I was reading the Scriptures—John 10:10 to be exact: 'The thief comes not but for to steal and kill and destroy but I am come that you might have life and that more abundantly.'

Weak and helpless though I was, when I read those words, it seemed an explosion took place within my spirit and instantly I felt God's healing power go right through my body, making me completely whole. In the days that followed my healing I met God afresh. I spent long hours in prayer seeking to learn God's design for my life and out of those days came a conviction which has never left me—*a disciplined daily prayer pattern is the highest priority in the Christian life.*

When I learned to establish a daily prayer pattern my ministry was transformed. I spent less time organising, planning and trying to motivate people but I found that the more I prayed the more was accomplished. And the accomplishments were deeper and more enduring than they were before. I achieved more by doing less!

The daily prayer pattern I learned to establish at that critical time in my life is something I want to share with you now. But before so doing permit me to reflect to you my basic concept of prayer.

I see prayer as self surrender. It is a commitment to develop a *relationship* with God rather than just asking him for *things*. In order to understand the deep significance of prayer, we all, I believe, must come to see that we have to die on one level in order to live on another. We must lose ourselves in order to find ourselves. This is the law of life that runs through the whole universe. The mineral kingdom surrenders to the vegetable kingdom and dead matter is turned into living forms. A person who does not surrender his whole being to God is like a branch which is not surrendered to the vine—lifeless and dead. A musician surrenders to the flow of music, listens to it, and pours it forth from his own being with complete and utter abandon. A scientist surrenders to the laws that govern the universe, flings open the doors of his mind and allows his senses to be guided by the facts. Those facts become forces which are gathered up and put to work for humanity in a thousand different ways so that humanity may be served.

It was *Kagawa* the great Japanese Christian who first introduced me to this thought. When asked for his definition of prayer he gave it in one word—surrender. This idea of surrender cuts right across the generally held view of prayer as a method by which we obtain our highest wishes and desires from God. 'Prayer' says a contemporary, 'is self realisation. It is the way by which we best realise ourselves and discover the person God wants us to be.' He is quite right of course, but before prayer can become self realisation it must be seen as self renunciation.

Everything from mineral to man has to lose itself in something higher in order to find itself. We respect the memories of men like Wilbert Wilberforce and Abraham Lincoln because they lost themselves in the cause of freeing the slaves from captivity. But in losing themselves they found a place in the heart of humanity from which they can never be dislodged. Whenever we put life under the microscope and examine it carefully we come out with one conclusion:

> 'Sweeter the strain when in the song
> The singer has been lost.'

Now I realise that some of course will object to my approach to prayer and say it is too passive. A denial of the will to live! Far from it. Self-surrender is the relinquishing of the defeated, empty ineffective self in order to find the level of a victorious dynamic and effective self. It is the petty self renounced so that the potential self might be realised. It is the wire surrendering to the dynamo, the flower to the sun, the branch to the vine. It is life surrendering to Life.

Prayer when it begins in self surrender is being true to the deepest law of the universe—saving your life by losing it (Matthew 10:39). You see it is perilously possible to offer prayer without offering yourself, but real praying means that the total *you* is praying. You give yourself to him and he gives himself to you. I see prayer then as a commitment to God, a self surrender, a giving of myself to him, not simply to get things from him, but because by the giving of myself I put myself in the way of getting all of God's best for me. In prayer God hears *me*—not merely what I say.

With these presuppositions concerning prayer in mind, how then do I go about my daily prayer pattern.

Firstly, I withdraw as soon as possible after rising, into my study to enjoy communion with God. Although my personality type is that of an 'owl' rather than a 'lark'—by that I mean I am much more alert last thing at night than I am first thing in the morning, I have learned the benefits of disciplining myself to establish what I call the *Morning Watch*. I do this because I have learned from experience the importance of turning the early part of the morning into a time of focussing on God. This was brought home to me whilst meditating on our Lord's vigil in the Garden of Gethsemane. After spending all night there in prayer he said, 'Rise, let us be going' (Matthew 26:45–6). I like my daily *Quiet Time* to end in the same spirit of saying 'Rise, let us be going'—to face anything, anywhere.

I found when I tried to fix my *Quiet Time* in the evening that it tended to be backward looking. When I fixed it in the morning, even against my natural disinclination, I came out with a tremendous benefit—it kept me forward looking.

Keeping this *Morning Watch* with God for me requires a good deal of discipline. I know that in some sections of the Christian church the word 'discipline' falls heavily upon the ear. Many Christians feel that now we are 'in Christ' we are not under law, but under grace, and therefore any talk of discipline is legalistic and unspiritual. To achieve power in prayer and to build and develop a rich personal prayer life discipline is essential. 'Character' said someone, 'is formed out of endurance'. For myself, the discipline of making a morning appointment with God and *turning up for that appointment* has developed more character in me than anything else I know.

Naturally there are times when I am unable to keep that morning appointment. Perhaps an early morning telephone call brings news of a family crisis, such as a serious sickness, or even a death. Things have to be organised right away. On such occasions there is time for no more than a few moments of prayer. But God understands and I am conscious that the One who loves me and has my life in his hands will see to it that although I have not had my *Quiet Time* I will not spend an unquiet day.

I find too, that using the same place for prayer—my own private study—has built up for me associations that call me to prayer even when I don't feel like it. The memories of communion with God come flooding back to me whenever I kneel in my room and it is not long before I discover as Oxenham put it:

> 'A little place of mystic grace
>   Of sin and self swept bare
> Where I may look into his face
>   and talk with him in prayer.'

Secondly, when closeted in my room, and before I engage in prayer, I prime the pump of my soul by reading from the Scriptures. George Muller, that great man of prayer, claimed that for many years he was defeated in prayer because he had not understood the importance of meditating in the Scriptures before approaching God in either petition or intercession. My testimony is something similar. Since I began to practise the art of meditating in the Scriptures before turning to prayer, I have discovered it to be one of the most revolutionary factors of my personal *Quiet Time*.

Usually I select a passage from the Psalms. This I find brings me into God's presence more speedily than anything. I see this exercise as letting God speak to me through his Word before I begin to speak to him through my words. It provides the right climate for the prayer time and sets my thinking in the right direction.

Next I read the Scripture passage for the day as set out in the devotional *Every Day with Jesus*. This is a daily Bible study guide I write, which follows a Scripture theme (or book) over a period of two months. I do this mainly because I want to keep in touch with the many thousands who peruse it, as part of daily prayer life is to intercede for them before the throne of Grace.

Taking time to read the Word of God before embarking on a time of prayer is in my view rather like a pilot tuning up his engines preparatory to a flight. The Word of God ignites my thinking, develops my spiritual aspirations and gets my prayers going in the right direction. This prepares me also to pray prayers that can be answered for they will be prayers that are aligned to the will of God.

Thirdly, after meditating on an appropriate passage of Scripture I still my mind in God's presence. This idea came to me when focussing on the text 'Be still and know that I am God' (Psalm 46:10). As I pondered that text I came to see that just as the moon cannot be reflected on a restless sea, so God cannot impress himself on an unquiet mind. When the Scripture says 'Be still and know that I am God' it is inferring that when we are unstill then we will not know God, for God cannot get to us.

Why do I seek to still my mind before moving into prayer? One writer says 'God not only answers prayer, but he also corrects prayer thus making it more answerable'. Just as reading from the Scriptures puts me in the way of praying prayers that can be answered, i.e. prayers in line with the will of God, so stilling the mind in God's presence reinforces this issue. I found when examining my prayer life on one occasion, that many of my prayers were shot through with self-centredness. A friend of mine, a preacher of the Gospel, told me that one morning he bowed his head in prayer and began with these words, 'O God, help me.' The reply he got from God was this: 'I will do better, I will use you.' He says, 'The amendment was decidedly better. I was asking God to help me—*I* was the centre. I was calling God in for my purposes. But "I will use you" meant *I* was not the centre; something, nay Someone beyond me, was the centre, and I was the instrument of a purpose beyond myself. God's answer shifted the whole centre of gravity of my prayer.'

When I still my mind in God's presence I give God a further opportunity to direct my prayers so that my praying will be truly according to his will.

Fourthly, I then begin to adore God within my heart. Adoration has been described as 'the creaturely bending of knee and bowing of heart before the Creator.' It transcends language, although language may be used. In adoring God I simply gaze upon him, allow him to fill my entire vision and think of the wonder that I, a soiled sinner, can come into his presence and linger as long as I like. This adoration then often leads to worship, to praise and to thanksgiving. Although the words adoration, worship, praise and thanksgiving are closely connected, in my thinking they are quite separate and apart.

I see adoration as contemplation—gazing upon God and reflecting on his goodness and his greatness. I see worship however as slightly different. In worship I believe I do more than contemplate his Person, but move out to honour him in sober words that express the homage of my inner being. Praise on the other hand means (to me at least) a *joyous* expression of one's delight in God where the words used are not sober (as when one worships) but lavish and extravagant. Where adoration and worship are mainly contemplative, praise is more vociferous: it means to shout, to extol and honour God with enthusiasm.

Thanksgiving I see as quite different from the other three words. Adoration, worship and praise is delighting in God for who he is. Thanksgiving is delighting in God for what he does. It is simply saying 'thank you' to the Almighty for his gifts and blessings and the good things of life. I believe for my prayer life to have a good strong foundation it must be based on a bedrock of thanksgiving. The Bible says, 'It is a *good* thing to give thanks unto the Lord' (Psalm 92:1).

Fifthly, after a period of adoration, worship, praise and thanksgiving I then pray for my personal spiritual condition. Many of today's great writers on the subject of prayer will disagree with me here and say that I ought to keep prayer for myself until last. The reason they give for this is that prayer should be guarded from all selfishness. This, I admit, is a strong and powerful argument. However, experience has shown me that when I pray for my own spiritual condition first the purification that begins in me then spills over into the prayers I pray. When *I* am purified then my prayers are purified.

At this stage in my prayer time one thought is predominant: How can I gain more of the mind of Christ? How can I become more and more like Jesus? I have reached the point in my life where despite all my experience, my training and understanding of people, I am increasingly conscious that I can be deeply and honestly ignorant of myself. Yet no real progress is possible without self-knowledge. Socrates—the wisest man of his age—greeted all his new pupils with the words: know thyself.

So deep is self-ignorance that we can be guilty of faults which stick out a mile in the gaze of all our acquaintances but of which we ourselves are completely unaware. We see the faults of others with great clarity. But not our own.

How then can we see ourselves? *How can I see myself?* I can only see myself as I really am as I gaze into the mirror of Christ. Christ is a perfect mirror. He reflects a perfect likeness of the image which falls upon him. Sometimes our friends and acquaintances tell us what they think about us, but they usually exaggerate our faults and speak in anger, so we toss their words aside. They fail to pierce the armour of our self esteem. And quite often too, those who are closest to us are blinded by their love and regard for us, and fail to see our imperfections. They bear with us for love's sake. What we all need is someone who sees into the very heart of us, love us deeply, but will never let us off. That Someone is Jesus Christ.

For a while then, I gaze into the mirror of Christ. I invite him to show me any faults, failings, or sins that need to be confessed and put right. Sometimes the revelation is appalling but I have learned that my faults and imperfections do not affect his love for me in any way or to any degree. He loves me as I am, but loves me too much to let me stay as I am. I am grateful too, that when I look into that mirror he does not allow me to see the truth about myself in one glance; it would be too much for me. He shows me a vision of myself in the measure I can accept. I am more than grateful that he allows me to see the truth about myself at all—and see it where alone it can be properly seen: *in him.*

If there are things that need to be worked on, such as an apology to be made to someone, a spiritual deficiency that has to be corrected, then I make a note of it in a notebook that I carry into the prayer time specifically for this purpose. I never go into my *Quiet Time* without that notebook. In some strange way it puts me into an attitude of expectancy. When I come expecting God to speak to me, the amazing thing is—he does.

Sixthly, my next task is to pray for others. I keep a list of people I know are in special need and from there I reach out into ever widening spheres. I call this 'praying in concentric circles'—first, family and friends, the community, the nation, Christian organisations, the readers of *Every Day with Jesus* worldwide, and other things the Lord might lay upon my heart. I have found over the years that the wider I have made my prayers the richer has become my prayer life. I have grown with the reach of my prayers.

At one time I used to go into my daily prayer session without any special prayer list, relying on the chance recollection of the moment. But this proved extremely unproductive. I came to see that probably nothing I could do for others was so valuable as praying for them and to do that effectively meant method. Now I use three prayer lists.

The first is my own personal prayer list. On this are the names of friends, family members, or people known to me personally who have either asked for my prayers or for whom I feel led to pray. Sometimes it may also contain the names of organisations known to me who are in desperate need, or who require persevering prayer. This prayer list is updated every week when I ask myself the question: Does the Lord want me to continue praying for these people (or organisations), or is he releasing me in accordance with his will, from further prayer responsibility? Sometimes I feel impressed to let some names remain and to continue praying for those people over the period of another week.

The second list is taken from the printed prayer programme of the *Crusade for World Revival* which is entitled—Prayer Focus. Every day the *Crusade for World Revival* draws the attention of thousands of people who are linked together in a worldwide Chain of Prayer to certain specific issues, for their prayer support and intercession. These requests vary from the inner cities of Great Britain to an almost unknown tribe in Central Africa. I find a great deal of pleasure in focussing my prayers on this particular list, for I know that perhaps at that very moment there will be thousands of people praying for that one particular prayer request. The feeling one gets from being part of this worldwide prayer link is something I am just not able to convey in words.

My third prayer list is one that I use just once a week— usually on a Sunday. On this list I put down the items which, although of great concern, do not I feel deserve a place in my daily intercessions. This list may contain items for which in times past I have prayed urgently, but now feeling a release in the Spirit to no longer intercede daily for them, yet at the same time feeling a need to keep them before me, they are then put on my weekly list. This list is updated once a month.

Intercession, asking God to bless others, I have found involves several important ingredients. First I ask God to help me in my imagination to put myself in the place of the person for whom I am praying. If it is not for a person, then I ask God to help me get into the heart of the difficult problem or situation. Next I focus my attention on God—his greatness, his might, his wisdom, and of course his accessibility through Jesus. Once I have a vivid awareness of God I then draw that awareness of God and the awareness of the need together in my heart. I hold them there for as long as I can in an attempt to fuse them together in the flame of believing intercession until God and the need become one. At this stage I usually pray *fervently*, claiming the answer by faith, giving myself to the situation as long as the Spirit directs. Properly employed, nothing is as demanding, yet nothing is as rewarding as intercessory prayer.

Next—the seventh step in my personal prayer pattern, is that of petition. Petition is asking God to meet one's personal needs. Here I differentiate between my personal spiritual condition which I talked about earlier and my physical, financial, or other personal needs. Petition prayer, I see as having to do with *things*. The intriguing thing about my own personal growth in prayer is that the longer I live the less time I spend in asking God to meet my personal needs. In the early part of my Christian experience, petition took up almost all of my prayer time. Now it occupies only a minor part; sometimes, merely a few seconds.

I have an ever increasing conviction that the more I ask God for himself, for the assurance that my will and his are not at cross-purposes, that we are in agreement on all major and minor matters, then I will get all the *things* I need. This is, I think, why one of the verses of Scripture that is becoming a favourite of mine is found in Matthew 6:33 where Jesus said, 'Seek ye first the kingdom of God and his righteousness and all these things shall be added unto you.'

I usually end my personal *Quiet Time* in the way that I began, by stilling my mind and giving God an opportunity to talk to me. This means that I let God have the first word and the last word—with me taking the middle word. I cannot conceive of a way of prayer that does not permit God an opportunity to speak directly to one's spirit.

'Prayer' said the late Dr W. E. Sangster, 'is conversation, and like all conversation, it is a two-way process. You talking to God; God talking to you.' I am amazed at the number of Christians I have spoken to concerning prayer who tell me that they give no time to the art of listening. If there is no listening side to prayer then we miss the real value of prayer. Far too many Christians come into God's presence and instead of saying, 'Speak Lord, thy servant heareth,' they say, 'Listen Lord, thy servant speaketh.'

As I wait before God in the silence, sometimes his voice is unmistakably clear. It comes as a gentle impression right into the soul. It is never strident. Mostly it is a whisper—a soft inner vocalisation that comes with clarity and conviction. If God, in the silence, says nothing, then I take it there is nothing—and rise to go about life's duties in the knowledge that communion does not always rest on words.

My way of prayer takes me about an hour to get through, sometimes less, sometimes more. It is not the only time during a day that I pray of course, for one can pray anywhere—in the street, driving the car, waiting for a telephone call to be put through, and so on. I see these unpremeditated times, however as *extras*—not substitutes. Any prowess that I have achieved in prayer (and God knows it is but an infinitesimal part of what it ought to be) is due in no small way to the establishment of a prayer pattern and the regularity by which it is maintained day after day. I believe that the most important activity of one's life should not be left to the vagary of feeling.

I confess that at times I drag myself to prayer feeling no inclination to spend time with God and with the needs of the world but, *whether I feel like it or not*, when I keep my appointment, it often happens that God rewards me with such a sense of divine immediacy that when the hour is up I can hardly tear myself away. Like the servant of Saul, I am 'detained in the presence of the Eternal' (1 Samuel 21:7, Moffatt).

My Path of Prayer

J. I. Packer

*The Rev. Dr J. I. Packer was educated at the Crypt School,
Gloucester, and Oxford University, where he studied
classics, literature, and theology. He is currently Professor
of Systematic and Historical Theology at Regent College,
Vancouver. He has been a tutor at Oak Hill Theological
College, London; a curate at St John's, Harborne,
Birmingham; Senior Tutor at Tyndale Hall, Bristol; Warden
of Latimer House, Oxford; and Vice-Principal of Trinity
College, Bristol. He has lectured in several countries (he
has held a Visiting Professorship at Westminster
Theological Seminary, USA), and is author of many books
and articles. He is married, with three children, and his
leisure interests include railways, jazz, cricket, and the
twentieth-century novel.*

THE INVITATION TO WRITE on 'my path of prayer' jolted me. That was not because prayer is in any way a freaky theme. On the contrary, it is central and crucial. I often begin talks on prayer by quoting Murray McCheyne: 'What a man is alone on his knees before God, that he is, and no more.' With McCheyne, I believe that prayer is the measure of the man, spiritually, in a way that nothing else is, so that how we pray is as important a question as we can ever face. Nor did the jolt come from lacking anything to say about prayer. In fact, a quarter of my book on Christian basics, *I want to be a Christian*, deals with praying, and it is a topic which no teacher of my type ever leaves alone for long. If I have trouble here, it lies in having too much to say on the subject; for just as a lot of theoretical knowledge about human relationships can breed a detachment which makes it harder to commit oneself to one's own family (whence comes distress sometimes in psychiatrists' homes), so a lot of theoretical knowledge about prayer, the activity which actualises our fellowship with God, can make it harder to commit oneself to wholehearted praying. I find I have to watch myself at this point. But that was not the problem which the invitation raised.

What was it then that jolted me? Answer: the little word 'my'. Was I being asked to describe how I pray on the assumption that I am good at it and might well be taken as a role model? That was not on. I would not want anyone to settle for praying as feebly, fitfully and ineptly as I feel I do. Also, my heart says that trying to describe what I do in prayer would be like telling the world how I make love to my wife. Parading such intimacies would be nasty exhibitionism on my part, and would pander to the unspiritual, voyeuristic interest in spiritual experience which is unhappily widespread today. To join the psalmist in telling what the Lord has done for my soul (Psalms 66:16) would be one thing, but to spotlight my own performance in prayer would be something else—a sort of spiritual strip-tease, entertaining perhaps but certainly not edifying. What then was I to do? I decided to write about the path I seek to follow when I pray, never mind how well or badly I get on, and that is my programme for the next few pages.

I start with the truism that each Christian's prayer life, like every good marriage, has in it common factors about which one can generalise and also uniqueness which no other Christian's prayer life will quite match. You are you, and I am I, and we must each find our own way with God, and there is no recipe for prayer that can work for us like a handyman's do-it-yourself manual or a cookery book, where the claim is that if you follow the instructions you can't go wrong. Praying is not like carpentry or cookery; it is the active exercise of a personal relationship, a kind of friendship, with the living God and his Son Jesus Christ, and the way it goes is more under divine control than under ours. Books on praying, like marriage manuals, are not to be treated with slavish superstition, as if perfection of technique is the answer to all difficulties; their purpose, rather, is to suggest things to try. But as in other close relationships, so in prayer: you have to find out by trial and error what is right for you, and you learn to pray by praying. Some of us talk more, others less; some are constantly vocal, others cultivate silence before God as their way of adoration; some slip into glossolalia, others make a point of not slipping into it; yet we may all be praying as God means us to do. The only rules are, stay within biblical guidelines and within those guidelines, as John Chapman put it, 'pray as you can and don't try to pray as you can't.'

Biblical guidelines for prayer are of two sorts. First, there are familiar *theoretical principles*, like these: Christian prayer is communion with God through conversation. It is an exercise of faith responding through grace to what one knows of the Father, the Son and the Spirit. It is prompted and fuelled mainly by three things: gratitude and adoration, which evoke thanks and praise; awareness of need, one's own and others', which calls forth confession, petition and intercession; and the desire, present in every regenerate heart, that God should be honoured and glorified, which leads to the kind of prayer that Scripture calls *extolling* or *exalting* him. The goal of Christian prayer is not to manipulate God into doing our will, but to further the doing of his will, in our own lives as much as anywhere else. Petition, based on promise, is the essence of such prayer, which is God's delight to inspire, hear and answer.

Praying, though from one standpoint the most natural thing a Christian ever does, since crying to his heavenly Father is a Spirit-wrought instinct in him, is always a battle against distractions, discouragements and deadenings from Satan and from our own sinfulness. Prayer is not easy, and although spontaneity is of its essence we have to make a dogged discipline of it, or else it would get crowded out—Satan would see to that! Should it degenerate into a formal routine, lacking inward concentration upon God and positive desire for his gifts and his glory, it would not be real prayer at all. Only through the energising Holy Spirit, who gives the awareness and desire from which prayer springs, the thoughts and words in which it is voiced, and the persistence in it which God commands, does prayer ever become all that it is meant to be; which is why Scripture summons Christians specifically to pray 'in the Holy Spirit' (Ephesians 6:18; Jude 20).

I said these principles are familiar. I wonder if I was right? Outside the evangelical tradition from which they come, contemplative rather than petitionary notions of prayer seem to prevail, and within evangelicalism a quietist stream of thought about communion with God flows steadily. Many often and gladly sing

> 'Drop thy still dews of quietness
>   Till all our strivings cease;
> Take from our souls the strain and stress
> And let our ordered lives confess
>   The beauty of thy peace.'

And many rejoice to read and recommend *Prayer*, by the Lutheran priest O. Hallesby, a book of which Donald Bloesch has justly written: 'Despite Hallesby's awareness of struggle in the life of prayer, the quietist, mystical element is more dominant than the evangelical one in his spirituality. Too often it

70

seems that for him the struggle is not an anguished cry but a painless surrender. The work of the Spirit is so emphasised that human endeavour seems small in comparison. Prayer for Hallesby is more a friendly colloquy than an unceasing battle. Although he speaks of wrestling in prayer, he makes clear that we wrestle not with God but with ourselves, with the distractions of the world. The essence of prayer for Hallesby is "an attitude of our hearts towards God", a "holy passivity" ' (*The Struggle of Prayer*, 1980, p 151).

I find the idea that God calls us to abandon, not simply self-justifying, self assertive endeavours, but all exerting of effort as such, and that responsive relaxation is always the only way to real intimacy with God and experience of his power, to be very common today. And that, I confess, bothers me.

In the mid-forties, as a new Christian, I tried to embrace this popular quietism as stated, found it simply unreal and nearly went off my head wondering what was wrong with me. Then I met the writings of the Anglican J. C. Ryle, the Puritan John Owen, and the reformer John Calvin, which showed me that biblical Christian experience, whatever else it is, is active battling throughout, inwardly against the flesh (Galatians 5:16:24), outwardly against the world (Romans 12:1f; 1 John 2:15–17), and in both against the devil (1 Peter 5:8f). Awareness and acceptance of the fight, they said, is itself a gauge of spiritual authenticity and vitality, and no Christian gets out of the second half of Romans 7 till he leaves this world. These authors also showed me at the practical level what P. T. Forsyth later theologised for me in his great little book, *The Soul of Prayer*— that God may actually resist us when we pray in order that we in turn may resist and overcome his resistance, and so be led into deeper dependence on him and greater enrichment from him at the end of the day (think of wrestling Jacob, and clamouring Job, and the parable of the unjust judge). So nowadays I reject teaching which promotes passivity, intellectual, emotional or volitional, as based on a misunderstanding of Bible teaching about faith and as being both unspiritual and unhealthy. I see true prayer, like all true obedience, as a constant struggle in which you make headway by effort against what opposes, and however much you progress you are always aware of imperfection, incompleteness and further to go. But I suspect this is a minority view. Let us proceed.

The second sort of biblical guidelines takes the form of *recorded models* of prayer—150 psalms, the Lord's Prayer, and the prayers of saints from Abraham to Paul.

Thomas Fuller said truly of the prayers in the Anglican liturgy that they are like big clothes which parents buy for their children to grow into, and the same can be said with yet more truth of the transcripts of holy hearts in action which these biblical prayers present. The Lord's Prayer in particular shows the pattern of goals and desires to which all truly Christian praying conforms, and I find it salutary to ask myself again and again: have my prayers spelt out what is in the Lord's Prayer? Also, I have found that to go through the Lord's Prayer, amplifying and specifying each clause (what the Puritans described as 'branching', and C. S. Lewis called 'festooning') is an infallible way to re-start when I get stuck, or when I am struck dumb by the feeling that all I say to God is empty and meaningless. (Does that ever happen to you? It has done to me.) As for the psalms, I am always intrigued to find how Christians relate to them, for it took me years after my conversion to feel at home in them. (Why? Partly, I think, because the view of life as a battle, of which I wrote in the last paragraph and which the psalms embody, took longer to root itself in my heart than in my head; and partly because the middle-class misconception that tidiness, self-conscious balance and restraint are essentials of godliness—a misconception which makes most of the psalms seem uncouth—possessed both my head and my heart for longer.) More and more, however, the psalmists' calls for help, their complaints, confessions of sin, depression, celebrations of God, cries of love for him, challenges and commitments to him, and hopes placed exclusively in him (all eggs in the one basket), have become the emotional world of my prayers, and I think this is how it should be.

So the way of prayer that I seek to follow can be described thus:

It is a *conversational* way. I am privileged to talk to God as a

72

man to his maker, a servant to his master, a son to his father, a friend to his friend (see John 15:13–16, 20:17).

It is a *trinitarian* way. I pray to the Father through the mediation of the Son and the enabling of the Holy Spirit. I may pray also to the Son and the Spirit directly when this is appropriate.

It is a *responsive* way, the human side of two-way fellowship. The triune God whom Christians love and serve communicates, as it were, by letter (the Bible), and we reply, so to speak, by phone (prayer). One day we shall see our Lord and speak with him face to face, but for the present our relationship with him goes on as described.

It is a way of *doxology*, that is, of giving God glory and worship; the desire to honour and exalt God and see others doing the same ('Hallowed be thy name') is at its heart.

It is a way of *two-tone address*, in which praise prompted by a vision of God (who he is, what he has done, what he will do) alternates with petition evoked by a sense of need.

It is a way of *exertion*. The Holy Spirit's help, without which we could not pray at all, does not make lifting our hearts to God and concentrating on him any the less hard work. Praying aloud helps, and history records that Puritans, Methodists and leaders like Charles Finney (to look no further) prayed when they could at the top of their voice. (It is, after all, only natural to raise your voice when you are pleading with someone, man or God.) One Puritan clergyman had a farm and a prayer room, where he prayed so loud that everyone on the farm could hear everything he said to God about them. We are told that this did them much good, but it is an example I would hesitate to follow. Let private prayer be private! (see Matthew 6:5f). Yet praying aloud certainly helps concentration, even if you only mutter.

It is an *energising* way. Spiritual alertness and confidence are the regular spin off from earnest prayer on any subject. The Puritans spoke of prayer as oiling the wheels of the soul.

Finally, it is a *rewarding* way, for recognisable answers to prayer bring joy and encouragement as nothing else does.

Four comments, now, to close.

First, a comment on *the Holy Spirit's help in intercession*. We should seek from God the requests to make in each situation, and recognise that it is the Holy Spirit's task, in addition to the rest of his ministry in our prayers, to guide us here as we lay facts before the Lord. Often we enjoy no special leading, and are only enabled to pray for needs in general terms, but sometimes the Spirit prompts very specific requests and leads us to make them with unusual confidence. Here, for what they are worth, are two personal instances. Once the theological college of which I was principal was to be closed by episcopal order. The community fixed a day of prayer about it. Two hours into the day, I found I knew exactly what to ask God for: a merger with another college on specific terms so controversial as to seem unrealisable. I could share this with no one at the time, but I held to the vision as best I could, and within a year all I had been led to pray for had happened. Glory to God! Again: a friend was in hospital for an exploratory operation; cancer symptoms were present. Many prayed. Laying the situation before God, I found myself drawn (for the only time in my life, so far) to pray specifically and confidently for a miracle of healing. Walking home from church on Sunday morning and praying thus, I felt I was being told that the prayer was heard and I need not continue to press it. On Monday the operation revealed no trace of cancer. Once more, glory to God! We must always be consciously open to be led by God in the things we pray for.

Second, a comment on *the link between meditation and prayer*. Meditation, which means thinking about God in God's presence, is a helpful preparation for speaking to God directly, and one which we seem regularly to need. In this world, interviews with persons of standing are handled with some ceremony, both out of respect for the persons themselves and also in order to gain most benefit from the interview. To rush to God randomly babbling about what is on our mind at the moment, with no pause to realise his greatness and grace and our own sinfulness and smallness, is at once to dishonour him and to make shallow our own fellowship with him. I, for one, want to do better than that. Like others, I find it good to preface my prayers about needs by reading Scripture, and thinking through what my reading shows me of God, and turning that vision into praise, before I go further. A little reverent thought about God before opening our mouths to address him makes a lot of difference to the quality of fellowship with him that follows. Remembering and reviewing who God is is never time wasted; it is, rather, a vital means of *knowing* God, just as prayer itself is.

Third, a comment on *the problem of supposedly unanswered prayer*. I say 'supposedly' because I challenge the supposition. While God has not bound himself to hear unbelievers' prayers, his promises to answer the prayers of his own children are categorical and inclusive. It must then be wrong to think that a flat 'no' is ever the whole of his response to reverent petitions from Christians who seek his glory and others' welfare beside their own. The truth must be this: God always acts positively when a believer lays a situation of need before him, but he does not always act in the way or at the speed asked for. In meeting the need he does what he knows to be best when he knows it is best to do it. The parable of the unjust judge shows that God's word to his elect concerning the vindication for which they plead is 'wait' (Luke 18:1–8), and he may say 'wait' to other petitions as well. Christ's word to Paul, 'my grace is sufficient for you, for my power is made perfect in weakness,' when Paul had sought healing for his thorn in the flesh (2 Corinthians 12:7–9), meant 'no', but not simply 'no': though it was not what Paul had expected, it was a promise of something better than the healing he had sought. We too may ask God to change situations, and find that what he does instead is give us strength to bear them unchanged. But this is not a bare 'no'; it is a very positive answer to our prayer.

As my eleventh birthday approached, I let my parents know by broad hints that I should like a full-size bicycle. They thought it was too soon for that, and therefore gave me a typewriter, which was in fact the best present and became the most treasured possession of my whole boyhood. Was not that good parenthood, and a very positive answer to my request for a bicycle? God too allows himself to improve on our requests when what we ask for is not the best.

And what do you make of this?

> I asked the Lord that I might grow
>   In faith, and love, and every grace;
> Might more of his salvation know,
>   And seek more earnestly his face.
>
> I thought that in some favoured hour
>   At once he'd answer my request;
> And, by his love's constraining power,
>   Subdue my sins, and give me rest.
>
> Instead of this, he made me feel
>   The hidden evils of my heart,
> And let the angry powers of hell
>   Assault my soul in every part.
>
> 'Lord, why is this?' I trembling cried,
>   'Wilt thou pursue thy worm to death?'
> 'Tis in this way,' the Lord replied,
>   I answer prayer for grace and faith.'
>
> These inward trials I employ
>   'From self and pride to set thee free,
> 'And break thy schemes of earthly joy,
>   'That thou may'st seek thy all in me!'

Or this?

> He asked for strength that he might achieve;
>   he was made weak that he might obey.
> He asked for health that he might do greater things;
>   he was given infirmity that he might do better things.
> He asked for riches that he might be happy;
>   he was given poverty that he might be wise.

He asked for power that he might have the praise of men;
   he was given weakness that he might feel the need of God.
He asked for all things that he might enjoy life;
   he was given life that he might enjoy all things.
He has received nothing that he asked for,
    all that he hoped for.
His prayer is answered.

Do we always recognise the answers to our prayers?

Fourth, and last, a comment on *the preciousness of partnership in prayer*. I have in view here not the wider fellowship of prayer meetings, scriptural and excellent as that is, but the special benefit of praying with a like-minded Christian who is committed both to God and to you. The Puritans would speak of the need and value of a 'bosom friend'—a person with whom you can share anything and do in fact share everything, and who can pray with you and for you in a way that ministers to you. In these days of relational awareness their point surely needs no argument. Everyone who has ever prayed with a 'bosom friend' knows that it is true. Happy then is he who finds such a partner, and stupid is he who never seeks one. In prayer, as in many other life-activities, it is good when we can travel two by two.

77

My Path of Prayer

J. Oswald Sanders

J. Oswald Sanders was a solicitor of the Supreme Court of New Zealand before joining the staff of what is now the Bible College of New Zealand. He was Superintendent for 13 years of his 20 years of service there.

He joined the China Inland Mission in 1946, first as Home Director for Australia and New Zealand, and then as General Director of the newly reorganized Overseas Missionary Fellowship from 1954–1969.

He retired from this exacting post in 1969 and has continued a worldwide programme of Bible teaching and conference ministry.

In 1973 he was appointed Principal of the Christian Leaders' Training College in Papua, New Guinea, where he served for two years.

He is the author of many books on practical Christian living and devotional themes.

In 1980 Her Majesty the Queen conferred on him the O.B.E.

IN A FEW PREGNANT lines James Montgomery has captured the heart of prayer, and distilled its essence.

> Prayer is the soul's sincere desire,
>   Uttered or unexpressed,
> The motion of a hidden fire
>   That trembles in the breast.
>
> Prayer is the simplest form of speech
>   That infant lips can try;
> Prayer the sublimest strains that reach
>   The majesty on high.
>
> Prayer is the Christian's vital breath,
>   The Christian's native air,
> His watchword at the gates of death;
>   He enters heaven with prayer.

Simple, yet sublime! Uncomplicated, yet complex! The artless expression of the redeemed heart, and yet the power that moves the arm that moves the world! These paradoxes of prayer find their solution more in the art of praying than in the academic study of the subject.

The growth of my own prayer-life has been marked by crises, large and small, in each of which some new aspect of prayer has opened up its secret. Prayer is the earliest cry of the new-born babe in Christ. The first evidence of Paul's new birth appears in the Lord's message to Ananias after the dramatic Damascus road experience:

'Go to the house of Judas on Straight Street and ask for a man named Saul, *for he is praying*'—and praying to the very One whom he had so recently been blaspheming. Thus began a prayer life that provides a model for Christians in all succeeding ages.

While there is no rigid and formal pattern for a life of prayer, in answer to their request, our Lord gave his disciples a model on which their prayers should be moulded—not a mere par-

rotting of a fixed formulary, but a personal adaptation of the
spiritual principles enshrined in it.

Each of us must cultivate his own particular pattern, for
what is helpful to one may be of no assistance to another. The
pattern may and will change with increasing maturity and
growth in spiritual intelligence. It has been so with me, and I
am still a learner.

Early recollections

The prayers of my immature youth consisted mainly of petition and intercession, and their scope was painfully narrow
and self-centred. I unconsciously tended to regard prayer as a
convenient method of inducing God to do what I wanted,
rather than as a means of his will being done in me.

A notable change came, however, when I saw that prayer
consisted of at least five main elements. With this new concept,
a whole new dimension in prayer emerged, for I realised that
each of these elements should daily find a place in a well-
balanced prayer life—*Worship*, the adoring contemplation of
God as he has revealed himself in Christ and the Scriptures;
Thanksgiving, the grateful acknowledgement of benefits and
blessings received; *confession*, the penitent acknowledgement
of sin and taking sides with God against it; *Petition*, making
request for our own needs; *Intercession*, our expression of concern for the needs of others.

My earliest recollection of prayer was when I was about five
years old. My parents used to attend an open air evangelistic
meeting after the Sunday evening service in the city of my
birth.

One Sunday evening, quite out of the blue, someone suggested that after the meeting, they should go to our home for
prayer. They all trooped into our lounge, knelt down and
began to pray. The Spirit of God came on the gathering and
they prayed until midnight—a totally unprecedented happen-
ing.

'Of course we are coming again tomorrow night' said one of
them And they did—and continued to do so every night for
three months, praying sometimes into the early hours of the

morning. Lives were transformed and some went to the mission field.

My bedroom adjoined the lounge and, child though I was, I can recall clearly the thrilling sense of the presence of God and the joyous singing. It was many years later that I learned that similar spontaneous gatherings had occurred in widely separated parts of the world about the time of the Welsh Revival of 1905–6. I cannot but feel that this evidence of the power and blessing of prayer coloured my subsequent devotional life.

After a transforming experience when I was about twenty years old, prayer became much more vital. But I found that really to worship God was an art difficult to achieve. My thoughts of him were very limited and rather stereotyped, and their expression monotonous and repetitive. A change came when I learned to use the Scriptures as a prayer-book, and to turn what I read, especially in the Psalms, into prayer.

I found the use of a good hymn book—especially one of the older ones that is rich in hymns about God, Christ, the Holy Spirit and the great doctrines as well as hymns of Christian experience. To begin the devotional time with meditating on a hymn or two was a most useful aid to prayer. Many of the great hymns are next door to inspiration, and we rob ourselves of much blessing if we neglect to use them.

Gifted men and women of God, in their hymns have expanded and elevated my thinking and expressed my deepest desires in language that kindled and warmed my heart. To think and pray through a noble hymn brings one into deeper fellowship with God. This is a Scriptural practice, for Paul asserts that one of the evidences of being filled with the Spirit will be 'speaking to one another with psalms, hymns and spiritual songs. Sing, and make music in your heart to the Lord' (Ephesians 5:19).

The Christian Book of Mystical Verse, compiled by A. W. Tozer has a wealth of such material. Take, for example, these lines from one of F. W. Faber's hymns:

O Jesus, Jesus, dearest Lord,
Forgive me if I say,

For very love, thy sacred name
A thousand times a day.

O wonderful—that thou shouldst let
So vile a heart as mine,
Love thee with such a love as this,
And make so free with thine.

Burn, burn O love within my heart,
Burn fiercely night and day
Till all the dross of earthly loves
Is burned, and burned away.

Who can read glowing words like these and not be moved to both adoration and aspiration?

In my early Christian life, the promises of the Old Testament used to be a problem. I had no difficulty in appropriating promises of the New Testament, for they were clearly made to Christians, but the promises of the Old Testament were made, in the main, to God's people Israel. It seemed to me that I had no more right to claim the fulfilment of a promise made to Israel, than to open and read a letter written to someone else.

C. H. Spurgeon maintained that 'every promise of Scripture is a writing of God which may be pleaded before him with this reasonable request: "Do as thou hast said".' But I found myself unable to do this.

The solution to the problem came when I read and understood Galatians 3:29. 'If you belong to Christ, then you are Abraham's seed, and heirs according to the promise.' God's promise to Abraham was that his descendants would be as numerous as the stars in the sky and the sand on the seashore (Genesis 22:17). He was to have a spiritual, heavenly seed, as well as a physical earthly seed—the earthly nation of Israel and the true Israel of God.

Through their union with Christ, who was Abraham's descendant, believers are indeed Abraham's spiritual seed, and as such are heirs to the spiritual content of the promises made to Abraham's earthly seed.

With the apprehension of this great fact, another milestone was passed, and I was now able through prayer to turn Old Testament promises into facts of experience.

Getting to grips with 'The Lord's prayer'

A further important prayer lesson came with a deeper understanding of our Lord's pattern prayer (Matthew 6:9–13). I had not previously noticed his warning against two perils that would beset the use of this prayer. We are not to pray like the *hypocrites* who reserved their praying for public occasions, whereas Jesus counselled them to use it in private: 'When you pray, *go into your room*, close the door and pray to your Father' (6:6). This prayer is not to be reserved only for public recitation.

Nor are we to be like the *heathen*, whose praying was a mere babbling, heaping up words without meaning (6:5,7). But it is not true that we do much the same when we repeat the form of words without intelligent participation?

It should be noted that Jesus did not say, 'pray in these precise words', but 'this is how you should pray'. He was not giving a rigid form of words, but a model on which our prayers should be based.

I was impressed by the fact that the prayer was half-way finished before any personal petitions or intercessions were even mentioned—a very different pattern from my prayers. This highlighted the fact that in prayer *God and his interests must have priority*. However, the divine order is not always the human practice. If God is not given his rightful place, our prayers will be anaemic. But when our thoughts are focussed on him and his interests, love is kindled and faith stimulated.

The pattern prayer taught me something else, for it indicates our sevenfold relationship to God when we pray. Here they are:

Father and child	—'Our Father'
God and worshipper	—'Hallowed by thy name'
King and subject	—'Thy Kingdom come'
Master and servant	—'Thy will be done'

Benefactor and beneficiary —'Give us our daily bread'
Saviour and sinner —'Forgive us our debts'
Guide and pilgrim —'Lead us not into temptation'

It can be a helpful approach in prayer to use a different one of these relationships each day of the week in our thought and prayer. This will impart freshness and variety to our praying.

The prayer also defines *the spirit* in which we should pray. Our spirit and attitude should be *filial*, 'Our Father'; *unselfish*, 'our' not 'my'; *reverent*, 'hallowed be thy name'; *loyal*, 'thy Kingdom come'; *submissive*, 'thy will be done'; *dependent*, 'give us our daily bread'; *penitent*, 'forgive us our debts'; *humble*, 'lead us not into temptation'.

It is a profitable but salutory experience to check our prayers to see if they really conform to the divine pattern.

The necessary prayer of faith

It was in a humbling way that I discovered how many of my prayers were simply prayers of *hope* rather than prayers of *faith*. Shortly after the close of World War II we were transferring from New Zealand to Melbourne, where I had been appointed Director of the China Inland Mission. We had no home to go to, and property was next to impossible to obtain. The returning soldiers had almost scooped the pool.

On arrival in Sydney en route to Melbourne, my wife and son of nine years old each prayed with me that there would be a home for us in Melbourne. When we rose from our knees, my son said, 'daddy, perhaps God has had a house for us in Melbourne all the time, but he has been keeping a secret!'

'Yes, perhaps he has,' was my unbelieving reply.

On reaching Melbourne, we were met by the secretary of the Mission who said, 'Alfred Coombe is going to England for six months, and he wants you to have his home while they are away.'

'There you are daddy!' exclaimed my boy. It was a humbled father who stood there. He had fervently *hoped* there would be a home in Melbourne, but it was not the confidence of faith. In the simplicity of his faith, the child confidently expected and even correctly anticipated the method of God's answer. It was indeed a salutary lesson. We must not be content with the prayer of hope, but persevere in the prayer of faith.

The reality of the help of the Holy Spirit in prayer, especially in the area of discerning the will of God, has been a continuing experience. Even Paul confessed that 'we do not know what we ought to pray,' but he added, 'but the Spirit helps our weakness' (Romans 8:26,27). As the Spirit of prayer, 'he intercedes for the saints in accordance with the will of God.' So long as he is ungrieved, he is able to guide us in our petitions, and to impart the assurance that what we desire is, or is not, in accordance with the will of God. He thus creates in us the faith that claims and expects the answer.

In prayer, distance from its subject is an irrelevancy. I learned this when travelling in China. We were travelling on horseback in a mountainous, bandit-infested area in the heart of the country. On reaching a certain spot, our escort warned that it was a danger area. We had proceeded only a short distance when we saw a dead body by the side of the track— apparently only recently slain, a grisly confirmation of our escort's warning. We were naturally very alert as we travelled on, but we negotiated the area safely.

Some days later I received a letter from my wife in Australia, recounting that one night she was awakened from sleep with the strong conviction that I was in danger. She rose and prayed for a long time until the burden lifted. On comparing dates and times, I found that her burden of prayer exactly coincided with the time we were passing through the bandit country. Our God is limited by neither time nor distance. He can lay a burden of prayer on responsive hearts thousands of miles removed from the scene of action.

Wrestling in prayer

Lessons in the aggressive side of prayer were learned through the exigencies of distressing situations, and seemingly insoluble problems. At a time when pressures were very great, I was given a booklet entitled, *The Authority of the Believer* by J. A. McMillan. He pointed out that prayer could be, on the one hand the expression of a restful faith, or, on the other, an intense spiritual conflict, as in Paul's prayer for the Colossians: 'I want you to know how much I am struggling for you' (2:1). Or in the case of Epaphras, 'who is always wrestling in prayer for you' (4:12). This teaching opened up a new dimension of prayer to which I was largely a stranger.

Our Lord delegated to his weak and failing disciples an incredible authority in prayer when he said, 'I saw Satan fall as lightning from heaven. I have given you authority...to overcome all the power of the enemy' (Luke 10:18,19). The unmistakable inference was that as they exercised this divinely bestowed authority, they too would see the overthrow of Satan in the area of their own life and ministry. The power of the cross is as potent today as when that epochal event happened, and that divinely-given authority has not been withdrawn.

This promise came alive in a painful recurrent situation. We had someone staying in our home whose almost demonic outbursts of temper made life almost intolerable. No line of action we took seemed to effect any improvement. In our distress, relying upon these words of the Lord, we prayed something like this:

> 'Lord, this present situation is not for your glory, nor can it be your will. We pray that your will be done here in this situation as it is done in heaven. We claim the fulfilment of your promise of authority over all the power of the enemy in this case, and we are trusting you to overcome the power of Satan in this person's life, and we do this on the ground of the victory you gained over Satan at Calvary.'

The result was almost incredible. So long as we maintained this position in faith, there were no further outbursts, and peace reigned. Since discovering this open secret, the effectiveness of this aspect of praying has been proved in many perplexing and often intractable situations.

With increasing responsibilities incidental to the direction of a large missionary society with global interests, and with widening interests and contacts, it was necessary to be systematic if important matters were to be adequately prayed for, so I drew up a two-week cycle.

There were, of course, certain people and situations that demanded daily prayer. Missionary interests were allocated in detail and by countries to different days. Various aspects of the work of our local church had their slots, as did my many friends around the world, some of whom were remembered daily, others less frequently. Then, of course, my own needs and commitments had their place.

Some may think this method is too mechanical, but it need not be so. A sanctified imagination can put flesh on the bones. Most of us need aids to memory, and I for one have found this helpful.

I can identify very fully with Paul when he confessed, 'not that I have already attained...but I press on... (Philippians 3:12). I am still very conscious that for me, 'there yet remains very much land to be possessed' in the realm of prayer.

My Path of Prayer

Phyllis Thompson

Before she became a Christian, in 1933, Phyllis Thompson had spent several years working in a correspondence school of journalism, and this early training seems to have set the course for her life in God's service. She went to China in 1936 as a member of the China Inland Mission and, although to do missionary work was her primary objective, her penchant for writing was recognized by the Mission leaders. Her first book, a flimsy volume of character sketches of Chinese Christians she had met, appeared in 1939. She was in China during the Second World War, and after a furlough in England returned there until 1951, when the whole Mission was withdrawn from China due to the pressure of the Communist regime. After that she was engaged for about fifteen years in editorial work in the China Inland Mission, and more recently has emerged as a free-lance writer of books for various Christian organizations. She lives in London's inner city, and in her eighties still finds most of her time taken up with writing.

Prayer to me is the primary means of keeping in touch with God. As the means of achieving my own ends, however laudable they may have appeared to be at the time, it has not proved invariably successful. There have, of course, been times when prayer has been answered in a striking, even a dramatic way, but it would not be true to imply that it has always been so. There have been occasions when it has apparently not been answered at all—not yet, anyway—or in a manner quite different from what I had expected.

Seven year olds can pray

The first time I ever really prayed was when I was about seven. I had a little friend, named Jean, who lived next door. She had blue eyes, a pink and white skin and fair, curly hair. Her mother used to put a blue band round her head, then slip a strand of hair through it on each side of her face, and she looked very pretty. I thought that if only my straight brown hair were done like Jean's, I should be pretty too, but my mother refused to do it that way. She put a band round my head, but said no, I was not to slip those strands of hair through it.

One day she sent me down the road to buy a loaf of bread. It was unusual for me to be out alone, and on the way back it suddenly occurred to me that now was the opportunity to do my hair the way I wanted. My mother could not see me and when it was done she probably would not notice. I squatted down on the pavement, placed the loaf on my knees and, tightly clutching the change in my hand, slipped those two strands of hair through the band round my head. Then I straightened myself, tucked the loaf under my arm, and opened my hand to make sure all the money was still there.

To my horror I saw that one of the coins was missing. The tiny silver threepenny piece, smallest coin of the realm at that time, had disappeared. In a hot perspiration of fear and guilt I looked on the pavement, in my other hand, in the gutter...the coin was nowhere to be seen. Then it was that I prayed. 'Oh, God, help me to find that threepenny piece!' I looked again, expectantly, but in vain. Eventually I had to give up the search and go home to confess to my mother how I had lost that threepenny piece.

My mother was very kind about it. She always was when we admitted that we had done wrong. But all that day a cloud hung over me in which there seemed no silver lining. My act of disobedience had robbed my mother of some money and, worse still, God had not answered my prayer.

That night, as I was undressing to go to bed, a tiny object fell to the ground at my feet. I could scarcely believe my eyes. There was the threepenny piece. I was almost speechless with joy and wonder. God had heard me! All that day his answer to my prayer had been hidden in my clothes.

I think I got the message too. He had answered my prayer, but not in such a way as to provide the cover-up of my disobedience. It was a lesson worth remembering.

Dawning realisation

Nearly twenty years passed before I really prayed again, apart from an occasional desperate inward plea on the tennis court that the ball might go over the net—a plea which seemed to fall on deaf ears.

By this time I was in my mid-twenties, a spoilt only daughter, with a marked aversion to anything and anyone connected with religion. However, paternal pressure to attend meetings on prophecy held periodically in the town hall resulted in my finding the subject rather fascinating, in an impersonal sort of way. Then one day it dawned on me that this great event to which the speakers invariably pointed, was really going to happen. Jesus Christ was coming back again. The realisation brought me up with a start, for I knew I was not ready to meet him. I decided I'd better do something about it.

Saying one's prayers by one's bedside at night was a common ritual fifty years ago, and I observed it, but now, to that meaningless rigmarole I added a definite request. I somehow knew that to be a Christian, faith was essential, and not having any I prayed, 'Oh, God, give me faith.' That was all. I didn't know what else to say. I also tried making a few minor reformations in my conduct, but felt no better and no worse as a result.

At what precise time my prayer was answered, I do not know. Like the threepenny piece that I'd carried with me all day without knowing it, faith appeared unexpectedly. After one of the meetings on prophecy I had a talk with the speaker, told him I wasn't 'saved' but was trying to be, to which he replied, 'Oh, don't try. It's all been done for you. Jesus Christ died on the cross to give you eternal life, and all you've got to do is to accept it.' This was news I had probably heard before, but it had never registered.

That night by my bedside, after some consideration, I prayed. My hesitation was due to the realisation that if I accepted this gift of everlasting life, whatever it might be, it would have to make a difference to my present manner of existence, and I wasn't quite sure I was willing for it. In the end I took the plunge, accepting the gift and asking Jesus to come into my heart, come what may. Nothing seemed to happen, so I went to sleep.

'I must be saved!' I thought to myself the next morning. 'I did what the man told me to do. I accepted God's gift.' I was rather surprised at not feeling any different from usual—no exaltation, no holy emotions, nothing. I was tempted to doubt the whole thing, but something within me encouraged me to keep on believing.

That afternoon during a conversation at a bridge party someone started talking about the state of the world, the threat of another world war and what would be the outcome. Suddenly she turned to me and said, 'Phyllis, what do you think is going to happen?' It was a simple enough question in a way, but I knew my moment had come. I had to give expression to what I believed. Suppressing my nervousness I said firmly, 'Well, I believe that Jesus Christ is coming back again.'

The effect of my remark on the bridge party was quite disturbing to the game, but its effect on me, myself, was as thrilling as when the threepenny piece fell out of my clothing. It was there, the real thing! It was no longer necessary to try to believe I had everlasting life—I *knew* I had it. 'For man believes with his heart and so is justified, and he confesses with his lips and so is saved.'

So started my spiritual pilgrimage, and the way of prayer.

Learning to pray

Probably few of us know what we owe to example and teaching. Whether I should have realised the importance of a daily tryst with God had I not known it was the habit of my father and other Christians, I cannot tell. Since I knew it was, and being assured that to go on in the Christian life it was necessary, I set myself to have one too. So I set out to learn to pray, by which I took it to mean speaking to God and hearing him speak to me, and put aside an hour early each morning for the purpose.

I will not attempt to describe the indefinable satisfaction, assurance, sense of stability that is normally the effect of these daily encounters. What a good nourishing meal does for a healthy body, the 'quiet time' does for the soul. It is the provision and preparation for the demands and duties of the day. I cannot honestly say that it has always been a joy, or easy to maintain, but I have not the slightest doubt that the establishing of that habit right at the start was of the most vital importance. It laid the foundation for all the following experiences in the inner life and for finding out, step by step, the path one should tread. Very early it dawned on me that God had a specific plan for me, that there was a way already prepared, and that it was my responsibility to walk in it. But could I walk in it if I did not know what it was? And how could I know what it was if he did not tell me? And how could he tell me if I were not near enough to hear him speak, if I did not get close enough to learn to sense, as it were, what he wanted?

Looking back over my life I remember very few of the innumerable prayers I have prayed during those set periods—prayers for guidance, for forgiveness, for strength, for needs as they arose and intercessions for others. The prayers that stand out most vividly are mainly those that have been condensed into a sentence or two, and one of those was uttered in the middle of the afternoon when I was sitting alone in our drawing room at home, reading a book. The book was about the experiences of three well-known women missionaries known as 'The Trio', and as I read of the beggar children, the desert dwellers, the vast unevangelised areas of north-west China, a deep compassion flooded my heart, different from anything I had experienced before. All those people, living in total ignorance of the love of a heavenly Father, of the provision he had made for them, of the home he had prepared! The longing to reach them with this 'good news from heaven' was so great that I flung myself on my knees and prayed one of the shortest prayers of my life.

'Oh God, for Christ's sake, send me to them!' I did not stop to think what unsuitable material I was for such a task, and evidently it did not unduly worry the Lord either. At any rate, he answered the prayer. Two years later I was on my way to China.

Two other prayers stand out in my memory, the effect of which I know to this day. One is summed up in the words found in Proverbs 30:8. 'Give me neither poverty nor riches...' I was afraid of the effect on me of either of those extremes and genuinely prayed to be steered in a safe, middle course. Inflation has accounted for what might have been the 'riches', while unexpected avenues of supply have provided the answer to the balancing petition. The second prayer, offered in the ardour of youth, when I feared my own strong desires might draw me away from the path he had planned, was 'keep me where you want me to be, even when its against my own will!' At the other end of life, living in a London borough I would not have chosen for myself, I am glad that God has honoured me by taking me at my word, because I meant what I said. We have to be honest with God.

There have been times, alas, when prayer has been hindered, when some sin in the heart has erected a barrier like a sort of glass wall, through which God could still be seen, but not touched, and petitions apart from penitence have been ineffective. One such occasion stands out very clearly. In my early years in China I had a young serving-woman whose main characteristic was not humility—so that made two of us. One day, noticing an undusted area in my room, I drew her attention to it, and when she flared up indignantly I reacted in style. The sparks flew to such an extent that my senior missionary was called in to arbitrate, which she did with grace and kindness, and things quietened down. Then it was I found that I could not pray. Try as I would, no prayers would come, and in the end I knew I'd have to admit to my serving-woman that I really ought not to have answered her back so angrily. Very shamefacedly I did so, and she took it very well, acknowledging that she'd been a bit to blame too. After that, of course, I found I could pray again. It was a salutary reminder that it is useless to bring our offerings to the altar until we have been reconciled to our brother.

Incidentally, my serving woman and I got on a lot better together after that.

———————

'Lord, I'm thirsty!' I was in a small Chinese town, off the beaten track, during the Second World war. My fellow missionary and I rarely saw another westerner, our supplies of books and Christian periodicals had dried up for parcels were not getting through, and I felt dried up too. Teaching, preaching, the round of missionary life had drained me, and I went to my room one afternoon in desperation. 'Lord! You said that "if any man thirst, let him come unto Me and drink"! Well, I'm thirsty, and I've come....' I did not know what else to say. I'd said all there was to say about my own condition, anything in the way of worship was beyond me, yet I knew I must stay in his presence, so to keep my mind occupied I decided to pray for my friends. I had a long list of those to whom my letters went, so got it out and started to pray for them. After about thirty minutes I folded up the list, got up and went on with my normal duties. Nothing spectacular happened, no exalted feelings came, but an hour or so later it dawned on me that I wasn't feeling dried up any more. Imperceptibly the waters had risen. Thirst was assuaged, and I could continue my appointed task again with quiet joy.

I have never forgotten that experience, which has been repeated many, many times since. The remedy for that 'flat' feeling has often been a time of intercession for others.

There seems to be something in this which I only dimly apprehend, even yet. It is not only that in seeking the welfare of others in prayer we forget ourselves, but that when we pray for them we are coming as close as we can to our Lord in his present ministry, since 'he ever liveth to make intercession....' In this way we are workers together with him, and since the consciousness of his presence is the sweetest joy we humans can experience, this is surely a way to obtain it.

That leads me to another aspect of the same spiritual activity which to me is, perhaps, the most satisfying of all. I cannot remember when first I experienced the special blessing that comes 'when two or three are gathered together in my name,' but I do know that down through the years what I have appreciated almost more than anything else has been fellowship in prayer with a small number of like-minded people. Our Christian faith is an intensely personal affair, and yet it can never be isolated. To reach its fullness it must be communal, as the Lord indicated when he taught us to pray not 'my Father who art in heaven', but '*our* Father who art in heaven'. The pleasure and excitement of receiving answers to prayer is clarified and intensified when we share them, but the great reward of those little group meetings for prayer for others has always been the consciousness of the fulfilment of his promise, 'there am I in the midst'.

Yes, prayer to me is primarily my way of keeping in touch with God and enjoying his presence. Even the fruits and benefits that derive from it, the guidance, correction, enabling for the mundane claims of my earthly pilgrimage, are of secondary importance to this.

My Path of Prayer

David Watson

*Having completed National Service, and a lengthy
academic training in philosophy, logic, ethics, metaphysics
and, finally, theology, David Watson was ordained in 1959,
and served his first curacy at St Mark's, Gillingham, Kent.
Three years later he moved to the Round Church,
Cambridge, where his burden for student work began to
grow. In 1965 he moved to St Cuthbert's, York—one of
twelve potentially redundant churches in the city and on
the brink of closure. After a slow start, God brought great
blessing, and in 1973 after the little church was full, with
television relays in another building, the congregation
moved to St Michael-le-Belfrey, opposite York Minster, in
order to accommodate the steadily increasing congregation.*

*He was later set apart as Rector of St Michael's, which
enabled him to travel and undertake mission work, usually
with the triple aim of evangelism, renewal and unity. He
became well known as an author, with over 10 books
written before his death. He and his wife, Anne, had two
children, Fiona and Guy.*

He died on 18th February 1984.

'WHAT A MAN IS alone on his knees before God, *that* he is—
and no more.'

Those words of Robert Murray McCheyne have both
humbled and haunted me down the years, like the hound of
heaven. Some Christians might know of me as 'preacher, evangelist, writer...' But what I really am, on my knees before God,
is quite another matter. Like many others, I need a strong grasp
of God's infinite mercy and grace to be released from a conscience which continually condemns me for my abysmal
failure in prayer.

Why, then, have I dared to respond to the invitation to write
about 'my path of prayer'? It is not, I can assure you, because I
cannot wait to share the secrets of my victorious and powerful
prayer-life! It is not to dazzle you with exciting stories of
sensational answers to prayer in the realm of the miraculous.
But if some are encouraged by the truth that God's power
'shows up best in weak people' (2 Corinthians 12:9) even in the
business of prayer, this chapter will not be in vain.

How it all started

I knew little or nothing about prayer until my conversion at the
age of 21. I remember trying hard from time to time, usually
with a sense of depressing unreality; and whilst in the Army I
remember waking up one morning with a splitting headache
after a drunken party the night before, saying, 'God, there
must be a better life somewhere!'

Whether that prayer was heard in heaven, I know not. But
within a year someone told me how God could become real in
Jesus Christ, and on my knees at Cambridge University I
prayed my first meaningful prayer by asking Jesus to come into
my life.

Encouraged by a number of Christian friends, I threw
myself into my new-found faith. I set aside 45 minutes before
breakfast every morning, missing very few mornings for many
years, spending about half that time reading my Bible and half
praying. It was a disciplined prayer-life from the start; and
looking back, I am so thankful for the guidance I was given to
do this. I made prayer lists, covering every day of the week. I

prayed for my family, for my close friends, for several I was trying to win for Christ, for many more who had recently found Christ, for some Christian leaders and missionaries. After a year or two, my 'time of quiet' increased to about an hour and a half each morning, often 15–30 minutes in the middle of the day, and about the same time last thing at night—although some nights I would wake up an hour later, stiff and cold in a kneeling position by my bed!

To begin with, however, I was extremely wary about corporate extempore prayer. I had never known that such an un-Anglican and un-liturgical thing existed! After resisting the pressure of Christian friends for some time, I went to my first prayer-meeting—and was thoroughly put off. One undergraduate gripped his chair with such fervour when he prayed (my eyes were wide open, taking it all in with considerable disapproval) that I honestly thought the poor man was constipated. Others mumbled inaudibly beneath their breath, some grunted and groaned, or kept on interrupting my concentration with 'Yes, Lord!' or 'Amen!' It wasn't my cup of tea at all. A few were astonishingly fluent, and I kept on wondering how on earth they managed it, since they did not appear to be reading their prayers from any book or piece of paper. I had much to learn! Not that I realised it at first. When a friend lent me a book called *Prayer* by O. Hallesby, I remember being startled that anyone would possibly write 143 pages about prayer, and I took a long time to wade through it.

Gradually some of my prejudices and misgivings were removed. I devoured books by Torrey, Finney, Andrew Murray and others, all of whom stressed again and again the primacy of prayer. I discovered the immense value of corporate as well as private prayer, and slowly came to accept the different styles of extempore prayer that had been so alien to me at first. I began to believe Charles Finney's words: 'Let me go into the prayer-meeting, and I can always see the state of religion which prevails in the church...Every minister ought to know that if the prayer meetings are neglected all his labours are in vain.' Ever since then I have tried to keep prayer as the foremost task in any work of God. Tom Smail once wrote, 'How much it matters to pray is the measure of what we are expecting from God.' Over the years I have seen this to be profoundly true.

It's the real thing

Looking back, my two years at theological college, Ridley Hall in Cambridge, were two of the most difficult years in my spiritual growth. I had been converted for only three years, was still unsure and immature in my faith, so clung tenaciously to what I did know and was deeply critical about everything else. Having discovered the value of disciplined private and extempore corporate prayer, I looked upon the formal daily chapel services as unhelpful intrusions in the patterns I had formed for my life. Mentally I would often 'switch off' and use the time for going through my prayer lists. I had not yet learned to be flexible, and was making those prayer lists into a legalistic and pharisaical ritual. Although reasonably faithful by my own standards, I doubt if the Lord was very pleased with me. My critical spirit must have made many of my prayers meaningless, but I was unaware of it at the time.

It was something of a surprise, therefore, when I began to see, quite clearly and painfully, that I had not yet 'arrived'. Through a careful study of the Beatitudes, God by his Spirit began to break my spiritual pride and complacency. To be honest, things had not always been as successful as had appeared on the surface. Although I had a wonderful curacy in a dockyard area (Gillingham, Kent) I had been seriously defeated in certain parts of my life; I enjoyed Christian work more than I enjoyed Christ; and I knew little of the spiritual dynamic that so obviously characterised the early church. I came to see that I was poor in spirit, and began to mourn for that fact. God made me meek, broken at the foot of the cross, and I became increasingly hungry and thirsty for God and for his righteousness.

All this was in 1962–3, which was before any 'charismatic renewal' in this country. However, I had been reading stories of revival throughout the history of the church, and I was soon praying most earnestly, sometimes for more than an hour at a time, that God would fill me with his Holy Spirit, and do something new in my life. This unusual state of spiritual hunger was a time when the Spirit of God touched my conscience about various aspects in my life which were not pleasing to God, and I came to a deeper repentance than I had known before.

One day, in February 1963, God gave me a gift of faith to believe the promise in Luke 11:13 that the heavenly Father would give the Spirit to those who asked him, I asked, believed and started praising God that he had answered my prayer— initially without any experiences or indications that he had done so, apart from his promise. After a time, however, I had a gentle sense of the love of God filling the whole room and overwhelming me. God himself became intensely real. I fell in love with Jesus. I enjoyed nothing so much as prayer, particularly praise and worship—which until then had always been something of a dutiful battle. It was an extraordinarily fruitful time evangelistically, too. I saw people won for Christ every week. I prayed much with other Christians as well as on my own. I became more aware of spiritual warfare. Indeed, the whole experience for me was a 'leap in reality'.

New patterns of prayer

This fresh release of the Spirit affected my prayer life in a number of significant ways.

Most important of all was an altogether new experience in the realm of worship. The most common word for worship in the New Testament (coming 66 times) could well be translated, 'I come towards to kiss'. With a new awareness of the love of God, I wanted to sing *to* the Lord, not just sing about him. I wanted to tell God that I loved him. My whole relationship with the Father was that of a son discovering consciously for the first time the depths of the Father's love: 'Abba! Father!' My relationship with the Son of God was best expressed by that exquisite love-poem, the *Song of Solomon*. Praise and worship became like the breath of heaven to me. Together with the grand old hymns which tell out the great truths of the gospel, I came to appreciate much more intimate worship in some of the gentle and simple songs, with their often repetitive choruses. Far from vain repetition, these became like a 'sung meditation' as I discovered what it meant to *enjoy* God's presence and to *delight* myself in the Lord. Often I use such songs today in private praise, as well as corporate. The psalms sprang into new life. I could understand why the psalmist said, 'Seven times a day will I praise thee.' This was not a duty, but a foretaste of God's glory. Still, today, praise and loving worship is the most important part of my prayer life.

After some theological and intellectual battles I also began to enjoy the gift of tongues. Like many other Christians I know, I had endless hang-ups about tongues. I was a dispensationalist and was quite convinced that all such gifts were purely for the apostolic age alone. However, after hearing disturbing testimonies from people like Larry Christenson and Dennis Bennett, I began to probe further and felt increasingly that my theological position had been no more than a rationalisation of why such gifts had largely disappeared from the church since New Testament days. After a struggle in which my intellect and pride raised many protests, I began to praise God in syllables that I did not understand.

Every time I analysed the sounds with my active mind, I found them rather unedifying, but when I used these syllables to worship the Lord, I found myself unusually refreshed in spirit. Language is basically a series of sounds or syllables which are vehicles of communication. In rational communication between two minds, we use sounds that we understand. But why should my spirit not communicate with God, who is Spirit, with sounds or syllables which I may not understand, but which are still vehicles of communication? 'Tongues' are not irrational, but trans-rational, or supra-rational. God is not limited to human rational thoughts, important though that is. There are many forms of communication between the believer and God: silence, 'sighs too deep for words,' intelligible words, songs, shouts, movements, dance, and so on. When my spirit wants to worship God or pray to him, a wide variety of expression can all be meaningful, including tongues.

I find tongues particularly valuable when seeking to abide

in God's presence, when tense or fearful, when tired or sick, when engaged in spiritual warfare, when trying to hear God speak, or when not knowing how to pray for someone for whom I have a burden. Sometimes I sing in the Spirit, letting the Holy Spirit use my voice in unrestrained adoration towards my heavenly Father. Often, after such a time of singing or praying in tongues, I am much more able to listen to God, and to hear what he is saying to me, either through the scriptures or just through the stillness of his presence.

There is also value in fasting with prayer. I'm not much of an expert at this—I still love my regular meals too much! But I have certainly known the value of fasting and praying when seeking the guidance or power of the Lord. When my wife and I first moved to York in 1965 we were faced with an almost empty church which would probably have become a museum within a year. What were we to do? Of course we prayed and preached and visited. But it was not enough. So we gave ourselves to prayer and fasting one day a week—every Wednesday—for the best part of a year. In effect we were asking: 'Lord, there are 101 good things we could try to do here; but what do you want us to do at this moment in time in this particular place?' We would begin each day with praise and prayer, then read the Bible together. After that we would discuss some aspect of the work for which we needed guidance. Then we would pray again, listening to God until we had a sense of peace about some issue. Sometimes God spoke through prophecy or through pictures we had whilst praying. Often it was through the general teaching of the scriptures. At times it seemed as though the Lord put into our minds some idea which we then pursued by more prayer and more discussion. We usually started at about 7.30 in the morning and went on to 3, 4 or 5 in the afternoon—by which time we sensed that the day's work had been done. They were extraordinarily rich times. Almost all the significant developments in the church in that first year came from those days of prayer and fasting.

I have likewise known the value of fasting before special evangelistic services, or when engaged in obvious spiritual warfare. Through missing a meal or two the human spirit is sharpened in its perception, the mind is less dulled, and the discipline itself is an indication to the Lord of the strength of the heart's desire. I am sure I have much more to learn along these lines in the future.

Present patterns and lessons

After many years of working diligently through prayer lists, I felt the need to escape—at least for a time—from the growing bondage of these lists. For several years I prayed for people whenever I thought about them, heard from them or wrote to them. That was a necessary spell of freedom for me. But about a year or two ago I felt I was becoming lazy and careless in my praying for certain individuals, so I have returned to some lists again, though am constantly altering and revising them. Perhaps the keynote here, in meaningful intercession, is variety. Use whatever method is a help to you at that time, without becoming a slave to any.

Variety in posture is also important for me. Often I sit at my desk, with my Bible and prayer lists open in front of me. Sometimes I kneel, to help concentration. Sometimes I walk around my room, or early in the morning around the streets. Walking and praying go so well together. Occasionally I use movement in prayer, lifting my hands in worship, holding (in my imagination) a sick person in my arms as I bring him or her to the Father. I have even danced in prayer, but usually in private! At times I take the classical sitting position for meditation: sitting in an upright chair, back straight, feet firmly on the ground, hands relaxed on the thighs. In this way I am able to release tense muscles, so that I can quietly meditate on a verse or phrase from the scriptures.

I am learning also not to be in bondage to any patterns of prayer. Although I personally find some discipline necessary— I still fight to get up early in the morning, and it is no easier now than when I first started!—I realise at the same time that if I happen to miss my usual time, the game is not up. God is the God of grace. My relationship with him does not depend on my faithfulness in keeping the rules I have set for myself. I have to learn to 'practise his presence' at any time of day or night. This is particularly important with the considerable amount of travelling I do at present. Rising early to catch a 7 o'clock plane in the morning from a busy airport, and later finding that I've gained or lost 9 hours in flight, thus throwing my interior time mechanism temporarily into confusion, calls for flexibility! In such experiences, praying in tongues; snatching a few minutes here and there with my Bible, talking to the Lord in any place at any time—all these are necessary lessons I'm learning in order to keep spiritually in tune.

At present I have no fixed pattern of prayer at night. Years ago I was struck by the sanity of a story concerning the great evangelist, D. L. Moody. During one of his famous campaigns, after an exhausting day, he retired to bed, and his host, curious to discover how this man of God prayed, tip-toed up to his bedroom and looked through the keyhole. He saw Moody put on his nightshirt, jump into bed, say 'Good night Lord, I'm tired!'—and go to sleep. Apart from the nightshirt I have often done the same. Sometimes, particularly on missions when I am preparing and giving numerous talks, I find that Bible reading late at night can cause my mind to go on preparing yet another talk, and sleep becomes difficult. So I read a novel instead. Usually after 2 or 3 pages, my eyelids become heavy and I sleep very quickly. Or else I read a psalm or two—or some other suitable passage—to settle tensions and anxieties that may have arisen during the day. Again, flexibility is the key.

There are other times, when I almost give up the battle of prayer altogether, and have to trust God's grace and faithfulness. This is particularly true during seasons of depression that I sometimes suffer from. The Lord seems a million miles away, and yet in the depths of that pit I know he is there (Psalm 139). I have no desire to pray, and cannot begin to worship, yet my heart is crying out for help. When we are depressed, tired or sick, I believe that God hears our innermost sighs and groans, even though we may feel unable to express these in words. It is at these moments that tongues again can prove most valuable. I am learning to relax in the Lord, to strive less and to trust more.

On other occasions we are meant to strive or wrestle in prayer. When engaged in spiritual warfare, when praying for someone's deliverance from demonic powers, when fighting against the 'spiritual hosts of wickedness' in evangelistic work, when interceding on behalf of a person, a church, a city or a country—then we need to 'stir up ourselves to take hold of God' (Isaiah 64:7). The great intercessory prayers in the Bible teach us the importance of this form of 'arguing' in prayer. Usually I find it helpful to pray with others for this purpose. We need to encourage one another's faith.

Listening to the Lord is extremely important, more so than talking to him. Both in our church and in the team I constantly travel with, we have 'sharing times'—almost every day with the team. After some praise and prayer together, we share with each other what the Lord has been saying to us or doing in our lives during the last 24 hours or so. Normally we refer to some verse in the Bible through which God has spoken to us, but we try not to make this just a 'best thought'. We aim to keep our lives open to God and to each other by sharing more personally. I may acknowledge, for example, that I am anxious about some decision I have to make, but the Lord has been reminding me about this or that. In this way we make ourselves vulnerable, but are often able to discern what God is saying to us, both personally and corporately. These are nearly always enriching times which enable our relationships with the Lord and with each other to be open and real. Our 'sharings' may not be immensely profound; but they help each of us to grow up together in Christ.

I am also learning to teach my heart to say 'I do not know'. I do not know why four young people with cancer, three of them parents, all died within months, when as a congregation we had prayed and fasted for them as we had never done before. I do not know why some are healed when prayed for and some are not. I do not know why violence continues in Northern Ireland, why famine persists, why rain is withheld, why natural disasters occur. But I do know that if I could understand all God's ways he would be no bigger than my mind and not worth believing in. I do know that the primary question to ask in tragedies is not 'why?' but 'what?'—'Lord, what are you saying in this?' Always he speaks to us in his love, however painful the experience may be at the time. I do know that in everything God works for good with those who love him (Romans 8:28). I do know that the Lord reigns. The best is yet to be.

Summary
With all these lessons I have been learning, is my prayer life now flowing smoothly? No, I am afraid it is not. In spite of all these realities in prayer, all too often I find myself too busy to pray, too tired to pray, too lazy to pray, too preoccupied with other things—Christian or otherwise. I can easily be the 'professional': preaching the truth without living it, not least in the area of prayer. And, uncomfortably, I know that is hypocrisy. Sometimes I feel dry in prayer. Often my mind wanders. On occasions it all seems desperately unreal. Nearly always it is a battle. But when, with the help of the Holy Spirit, I press through the natural reluctance to pray (which we all experience), I experience time and again the renewing love of the Lord. Certainly I have nothing to boast about, and much to confess with shame. I have anything but arrived.

Yet I do know that despite my miserable failures in prayer, all of which are without excuse, God loves me just as I am, God delights to hear my prayer, and God answers when I call upon him. God also goes on caring deeply for me, even when I do not care to pray to him. That is why I still come to him, and will always do so.

'I love the Lord, because he has heard my voice and my supplications. Because he inclined his ear to me, therefore I will call on him as long as I live' (Psalm 116:1).

My Path of Prayer

Jean Wilson

*Jean Wilson is managing director of Gospel Light
Publications, and has many other interests helping
organizations in the field of bookselling and overseas
missions. She attends St Paul's Church, Robert Adam
Street, London, where she teaches Sunday School children,
and she is also the Church treasurer. Among booksellers she
is well known as one of the founder members of the
Christian Booksellers Convention, which organizes an
annual exhibition for Christian publishers and retailers.
The exhibition attracts interest from all round the world,
and is a gathering place for all those in the field of
Christian literature.*

MOST OF US FROM time to time have posed the same question as the disciples asked of Jesus when they said 'Lord, teach us as John also taught his disciples.' It seems that for most of us prayer is one of the most difficult areas of the Christian life.

Most of my work is spent with Christian education and in dealing with young children. I never cease to be amazed how much insight these young people have into the spiritual questions which baffle adults. When asked the question 'what is prayer?', one eight-year old replied 'prayer is talking with God about everything.' A very simple answer on the face of it and yet a very profound comment. Talking is a very basic means of communication. We do not talk without expecting an answer. We do not talk without having to listen. Talking is a leisurely occupation. We talk when we want to tell someone of our very innermost thoughts. We talk when we want to find out about the other person. We talk when we enjoy being with someone.

When we think of prayer in these sorts of terms, it then becomes easier for us to see prayer as a vital part of our everyday lives, as we pray out all our plans, our ideas, our thoughts, in conversation with our Creator.

Yet prayer is much more than that. Most of us want God to answer our prayers in the way that we want them answering and not as the answer often turns out. Many times I have prayed that God would answer my prayers when I had already made up my mind what the answer should be. Then came God's reply and I found it very difficult to be obedient. George MacDonald put it so well in his poem *'Obedience'*:

> I said: 'Let me walk in the fields.'
> He said: 'No, walk in the town.'
> I said: 'There are flowers there.'
> He said: 'No flowers, but a crown...'

> I said: 'But the air is thick,
> and fogs are veiling the sun.'
> He answered: 'Yet souls are sick,
> And souls in the dark undone...'

I cast one look at the fields,
Then set my face to the town;
He said: 'My child, do you yield?
Will you leave the flowers for the crown?'

Then into his hand went mine;
And into my heart came he;
And I walk in a light divine
The path I had feared to see.

When we learn to accept God's answers then we learn the happiness of true obedience.

Another aspect of prayer that many of us find hard is learning to pray about something and then leave it in God's keeping. I learned this the hard way many years ago when I was telling a friend that I had been puzzling over a particular problem I was facing and that it had been causing me many sleepless nights. I can remember vividly the advice that I was given. 'Do you not believe the Scriptures?', my friend said. I was taken aback and replied very dogmatically, 'of course I do.' 'Then do you not believe 1 Peter 5:7'; my friend said, 'casting all your care upon him for he careth for you.' 'Well of course I do,' came my reply. 'Do you believe Psalm 121:4?', came the persistent question. 'Behold, he that keepeth Israel shall neither slumber nor sleep.' By this time I was getting rather incensed and once again replied that of course I believed in the Scriptures. 'Then,' my friend said, 'what is the point of two of you staying awake all night worrying about the problem?' The wind was completely taken out of my sails and I realised the force of that argument. From that day to this I can say that although I have had many problems and anxieties facing me, I have never been kept awake at night worrying about my problems as I now pass them all over to the Lord before I sleep. Of course I still have problems and difficult decisions to make, but no longer do they prevent me from going to sleep at night.

For the Christian, prayer is a great privilege as well as a responsibility. In dealing with young children, prayer becomes a great responsibility when you have many young lives to pray over. It came as a shock to me one day to realise that of the eight children I had in my Sunday School class at that time, six of them were from non-Christian homes and I was probably the only person in the world who was praying for those children by name. But with the responsibility comes the great privilege of sharing the needs and desires of those young children with their heavenly Father.

Children's prayers are so simple and direct. When a young child strokes the soft feathers of a bird and realises that God made the tiny creature he is holding, then this is a prayer of praise in itself.

In dealing with children in Sunday School the best times of prayer and praise are those that come out of experience. So often we tend to start our Sunday School sessions with 'worship' when the children are in a very rough and tumble state of mind. Football, new clothes, new additions to the family and yesterday's TV programmes all crowd into a young person's mind and suddenly to say to them, 'Now we are going to worship' is a vain hope. I find that to let the lesson continue with all its activities and ideas to complement and reinforce the aim of that particular Sunday, will result in the class being able to worship out of the experience gained.

Let me illustrate...you are teaching a lesson on the Good Samaritan and thinking of ways in which we can help people in day to day life and ways in which other people help us. As you proceed you begin to work out plans for immediate help and to acknowledge gratitude to those who serve the community...doctors, nurses, school teachers, policemen, etc. by having the children write a prayer poem. Perhaps you have decided to write a song of thanks to a familiar tune. Now we come to worship and we have the outlines of a great worship programme.

First, the children can praise God for giving them people to care for them, using the song they have composed as a hymn of thanksgiving.

Praying for forgiveness for not helping others themselves can follow and, in sharing what they have done in the lesson by reading their poems, a real spirit of prayer can follow out of their own experience. This is so much more exhilarating and exciting than for the leader to open the proceedings with set prayers and hymns, as the children are sharing their own thoughts and feelings.

I like to think of prayer not as something that one practises at specific times of the day, but as the very breath of life itself. Every act we do and every thought we think is bathed in a continual communion with God. Of course one does need to set aside certain times of the day for more concentrated conversation with God, but, nevertheless, at all times we can be in touch with him. I find that driving my car on long distances affords very great opportunities for prayer. There is a lot of time to talk and listen.

Many of us have experiences like Rhoda in Acts, chapter 12. Rhoda, you will remember, was in a prayer meeting with many who had gathered together to pray for the release of Peter from prison. When Peter knocked on the door of the house and Rhoda went to answer the knock, she was so amazed to see him there that she left him standing on the doorstep while she rushed in to the rest of the company, who immediately proclaimed her mad. The Authorised Version goes on to say that when they opened the door 'they were astonished'. What a great commentary on the response of many of us when God answers our prayers. We are so astonished that we fail to recognise that indeed our prayers have been answered.

The Bible is also very specific about our need to make time for our private, more concentrated, prayer and my own way of doing this is to set aside a period each evening before I go to bed. So many books that I read when I was younger concerned me greatly when they suggested that the best time for private prayer was early in the morning. I am not a person who functions very well early in the morning and I found that I could not concentrate to any great degree, even though I got up well ahead of the alarm clock! This was quite a battle for me in my younger days as I had great guilt feelings that somehow I was failing in my Christian life. Incidentally, when we read the lives of great Christian saints of the past who got up at 4 a.m.

for their prayer time, it is worth noting that in their day of no electricity they probably went to bed at 8 p.m.!

However, I came to realise that it was not the time of day that mattered, but the fact that a proportion of each day was set aside so that one could be alone with God at that time. My evening prayer times have become more and more meaningful to me the older I get. In the quiet of the evening, when all the cares of the day have been unravelled, and before I finally drop off to sleep, I find the time very conducive to prolonged and contemplative prayer. There have been many times when I have been facing some great decision in life that I have found the presence of the Lord especially real during those periods. On several occasions I have almost felt that were I to reach out I could touch him. Several instances spring to mind, but let me share just one of them with you. Some years ago I was in the United States and had been sent for a routine medical examination, only to discover that I needed to have surgery. That night in my hotel room I spent some considerable time talking with the Lord and especially as I was several thousand miles away from home amongst, almost, complete strangers. As I was praying I felt a great peace come upon me and again the impression that there was someone in the room with me. I then read my Scripture Union passage for the day, which took on a very special meaning for me. At the time I remember thinking that it was a most unusual book in which to find any kind of comfort as I was reading that day from Job 5:17–19. 'Behold, happy is the man whom God correcteth: therefore despise not thou the chastening of the Almighty; for he maketh sore, and bindeth up: he woundeth, and his hands make whole. He shall deliver thee in six troubles; yea, in seven there shall no evil touch thee.' What a promise to go with me as I went into hospital the next day.

A prayer notebook is very helpful in noting down those things for which I pray. Ticking them off when they are answered reminds me of my need to thank God for answered and unanswered prayers. The latter is a problem we all have to face. Seemingly so many of our prayers go unanswered but I have found so often as I look back over a particular situation that although I haven't received a specific answer to my request, yet in the very unanswered situation I have received the right guidance. That can be very difficult to accept but leads into a field of prayer which can be neglected privately and that is confession.

Someone had said that true confession starts with profession. That is to acknowledge the divinity of Christ and must be the outcome of our own deeply held conviction that he is the source of our own hope and salvation. When we acknowledge this, then we can see how far short we have fallen below God's standards and how many sins we need to ask forgiveness for committing or leaving undone.

Corporate prayer too is very important in the life of the Christian and I recommend the local church prayer meeting which can bolster and uphold each member of the church family. Perhaps the hardest part of prayer is constantly to praise when things are going wrong. So many instances spring from Scripture on this point and it is something of which I am having frequently to remind myself. Paul and Silas sang praises to God when they were imprisoned in the dark dungeon in the Philippian prison. Job had a hard time. He watched all his possessions disintegrate before his eyes and yet he could constantly praise God. In more modern times an event stands out when reading the experiences of Corrie ten Boom as she was imprisoned in Ravensbruck Concentration Camp. She and her sister discovered that the hut to which they were assigned was infested with fleas and her sister encouraged Corrie to thank God even for the fleas. It was a blessing in disguise as the guards did not bother the prisoners in that particular hut and they were able to continue with their Bible studies. Even in seemingly futile situations we can often find as we look back that God has indeed been with us and that we can priase him 'even for the fleas'.

I have to confess that I find it easiest to praise God in the countryside, with the beauty of nature all around me. It then becomes easy to thank God for all his creation. But I happen to live in the concrete jungle of London, surrounded by huge buildings and brick walls. I have to force myself to look around me and to thank God amist the evidences of man's ugly monstrosities and see God's creation even there.

I stop to admire the flowers that bloom in the window boxes, the sparrows that constantly hop on the pavements, the pigeons in Trafalgar Square and, on those nights when they are visible to watch, the stars in the sky. There are plenty of things around us for which we can praise God.

Prayer doesn't come easy, but I have always found that by making it a routine in my life, it ceases to become routine and is something that I really look forward to as I end each day, but, above all, I want to feel that I am praising God throughout the day in everything that I do, so that prayer becomes as natural to me as breathing.

My Path of Prayer

Richard Wurmbrand

*Richard Wurmbrand was an author and lecturer, and taught Old
Testament history in Bucharest, Romania, prior to the
Communist takeover. In 1945 he began a secret 'underground'
ministry—to captive Romanians and to Soviet soldiers in the
invasion force, and, despite the fact that he and Sabina were
both Jews and had lost most of their families to the Nazi
invaders, they also gave refuge and help to the German soldiers
who had fallen prey to the Russians.*

*Imprisoned from 1948 to 1956, he served three years in
solitary confinement and five additional years in 'mass cells'
during which time he was subjected to medieval tortures.*

*Following his 1957 release, Pastor Wurmbrand resumed his
underground work. Rearrested in 1959, he was sentenced to 25
years in prison. A general amnesty in 1964 brought his release—
and resumption of his underground work. Finally in 1965, in
great danger of a third arrest and imprisonment, he was
'ransomed' out of Romania by friends in Norway.*

*Today Pastor Wurmbrand directs all his energy towards
helping the suffering church in Communist-ruled lands. He is
the founder of Christian Missions to the Communist World.*

*He speaks 14 languages fluently and has written eleven books
since he has been in the United States, the most widely known
being* Tortured for Christ.

YOU SUFFER. ALL MEN DO. Very many are greatly grieved. Their real sorrow is even bigger than their feelings of sadness and despair and their reason can comprehend.

The other contributions to this book contain many interesting experiences in prayer by men who lead a normal life. But for some of us life is anguish, perplexity, darkness, unbearable burdens. Having suffered terribly from early childhood, and brokenhearted about many things even now, I will share what I know about prayer *in these circumstances*.

It is all but impossible to portray the degrading conditions of a Communist jail. We were literally in the depths—in a subterranean jail under the main square of Bucharest, capital of Romania.

We were segregated in solitary cells, abandoned to the isolation of our thoughts, without anyone with whom to share them, without books, paper, pencils, without even a tiny window into the sights and sounds of the natural world. For us no sun shone, no bird sang, not even a weed blossomed.

We were unspeakably hungry. At times we were allotted only one slice of bread a week in addition to our daily soup of dirty potato peelings or cabbage with unwashed entrails.

To break our resistance, we were tortured and beaten.

Beyond that, we were doped. In the prison 'coffee' and soup there were drugs to destroy the mind. As a result, in time we lost our memory.

Once I had known many languages. Now I could scarcely find the right words even in my native Romanian tongue. I forgot all theology and all the books I had ever read, including my own. Then I forgot the Bible.

One evening, as I tried to recite the Lord's prayer, I realised to my dismay that I had forgotten it. 'Our Father which art in heaven,' I prayed, 'hallowed be thy name. Thy—'. Here I stopped, my mind a blank. I could not continue.

I was very sad. The Son of God came from heaven to earth to teach us this prayer, so it must be important to know it. What would I do now that I had forgotten his words?

Very soon a comforting thought came. I had forgotten the

prayer, but I knew *which* prayer I had forgotten: one beginning with the assertion that he who rules heaven is my Father. I need not worry. Folding my hands I said, 'Our Father which art in heaven, I have forgotten the prayer, but surely by this time you know it by heart. You have heard it so many times. Consider that I have said it. I love you. Amen.'

The hunger became more and more nagging. The doping continued. Our minds no longer functioned. For a long time, I, along with other prisoners, could only say, 'Jesus, I love you.' To give him pleasure I said the words in Hebrew. This much I remembered: *'Yeshua, ani ohev otha.'*

I have been married forty-five years. Several times a day I tell my wife that I love her. She never once told me she was annoyed at my words. Neither did I have the feeling that Jesus was bored with the repetition of this simple prayer.

But the doping and the hunger worsened. We were mere skeletons. It became hard to say even these few words. I had to abandon prayer altogether. Or rather, I never abandoned it. There was nobody with the power to decide that praying should cease. I willed nothing. Prayer simply stopped, unless God counted as prayer the simple beating of a heart that loved him.

Other prisoners near me—as I found out later—had had similar experiences.

In my case, the blackout of the mind lasted some two years. After that, the doping ceased abruptly. There was also an improvement in the food.

Slowly...slowly...parts of my mind came back. Music and mathematics remained forgotten forever, as did many other things. In time, however, small pieces of the Bible emerged, though I could not connect them well.

One day I discovered that I could say again the 'Our Father'. It was like awaking out of a swoon. Every word was new to me and full of depth.

'Our Father.' My father had four children. I was the youngest and also always the weakest, often sick. My father had more sympathy for me than for the others. If God is our Father, then I can trust him even if I am the one who has sinned the most.

119

'Our Father.' That means that I, like the child of an earthly parent, am a kind of reproduction of him. Da Vinci's 'Last Supper' would have affected very few if not for its many reproductions. The manuscripts of the Bible would have helped few find salvation if they were not reproduced in millions of copies. God would be unknown if it were not for his Son, 'the express image of His glory,' and for his many children—millions of them—who reproduced his traits.

'Our Father.' When we were in common cells, often, very often, I heard Christians praying this prayer, slowly, savouring every word as if it were new to them. The recitation of a prayer was prolonged like Gregorian chant in Orthodox churches or the music of the Hasidic synagogue.

There was no reason to rush from 'Our Father' to the next words. It was enough to know that I had a Father. It was my duty to pattern my character after this model, never satisfied with what I had already attained.

A Greek painter once exhibited a picture of a boy with a bunch of grapes so lifelike that birds flew down to peck at them. He was eagerly acclaimed as a master-artist. He demurred. 'If I were,' he said, 'the boy would have kept the birds away.'

There is much refining to be done after every word of prayer. What is the good of prayers hurriedly spoken? We were thankful to the communists, who had provided us with one of the most important ingredients in prayer: time.

As our mental acuity gradually increased, we were happy to spend whole nights in prayer. Some fasted three or four days a week. (We had not much to eat anyway.) We prayed for every land and town whose name we recalled. We prayed for every single person whom we remembered, even for those evoked in fantasy.

For a long time we had forgotten. Now we were able to say again, 'hallowed be thy name.'

Though the guards were not allowed to speak to us privately, they often did. Some were converted. Since we had very little occasion to converse, we quickly taught them the main tenets of faith and the Lord's prayer.

A new-born guard, hastily instructed, inquired of the one who brought him to salvation, 'I cannot be a parrot. When I ask that a name be hallowed, I must know what this name is. What is the name of God?'

What is the Name?

Previously, when we were free, we spoke words like 'God', 'the Father', 'his Name', 'Jehovah' casually, often without reverence. How unlike the Jewish scribes who, even now, when they write the scroll of the Law for the synagogue, immerse in waters of purification as often as they come to one of his names. They might bathe as often as fifty times a day.

Now we felt the same reverence. It would take some Christians ages to say 'Our Father..., hallowed be thy Name.' Spurred by guards who inquired about God, we would ask ourselves questions about the Name for whose sanctifying we had so often prayed.

My fellow-prisoner, in response to the convert, replied, 'God has all names, including yours and mine. He is the God of Abraham, Isaac, Jacob, and of all godly men.'

After such an illumination, we prayed 'hallowed be thy name' as if to say, 'hallowed be the name of John, Peter, Joan, Magdalene, Georgette, Alex, Amelie...'. We had before us thousands of faces bearing the name of God.

There was almost no time left for any other prayer than the 'Our Father'.

But did we not pray for our release or for the easing of our privations?

At the beginning many of us did. First I was in a jail in which we were guarded not only by men, but also by dogs, large German shepherds. They conducted us as readily to the washroom as to our interrogations. They were perfectly trained to jump at the throat of a prisoner but never to bite. Their barking would awaken us from sleep.

At that time I prayed the Lord's prayer up to the words '*Thy* will be done on earth, as it is in heaven.' Here I would add, '— except for the question of the dogs. Here *my* will must be done. Please free me from the dogs.'

I was very pure that 'all things work together for good,' all things except for the presence of the dogs in the corridor. How human it is to feel that all things work together for good—except the one thing that bothers me most.

It took me a while to get to the point where I could say only, 'Thy will be done.' After this, I was moved to another prison.

Obviously, we did not all have the same prayer experiences. But while most of us presented to God our daily needs, I know several of us soon abandoned prayers for release or for improvement in treatment.

There were times when the Lord was so near one could almost touch him. On those blessed occasions he would ask clearly, 'Richard, is it too difficult for you?' And I would reply, again and again, 'Look after the others, I can bear it.' I felt very happy in those moments.

I cannot boast, though, that this was a permanent state. There were moments of despair, of unbearable separation and doubt, but somehow these did not belong to the essence. It is difficult to explain, but I will try.

Surely every man is more important to himself than his prayer. It is for this reason that prayer encounters so many hindrances. I am also more important than my feelings of elation or sadness, or nearness to the Lord or rejection by him.

In actions, feelings and thoughts there are many variations, but my real self is not in them. I am sad but also sad about my sadness. At other times I am joyous and even more joyous about being joyous.

Prison life helps one plumb the depths of human experience. Unlike most free men, we penetrated to the bottom layers of personality where, as Jung says, the immemorial archetypes live. I would call it the 'thick darkness' in which God dwells (1 Kings 8:12). There we had quiet and serenity even in moments of blank despair.

Probably the fact that I am Jewish has helped me. When I said, as I did very often, 'Eli, Eli, lama sabachthani (My God, my God, why hast thou forsaken me)?' I knew that the word sabachthani, like many Hebrew words, has two opposite meanings: to forsake and to glorify. The words could as well be translated, 'my God, my God, to what extent have you glorified me?' The Therapeutes, a division of the Essene sect, ended their daily prayers with these words as an expression of joy, like 'hallelujah'.

In prison I knew some Christians—not many, it is true—for whom the thinker, the thought, and the One thought of in prayer melted into one. In their transfigured faces, which inspired awe even among the guards, a great biblical secret was revealed. It is contained in Isaiah 44:6: 'I am the first, and I am the last' (in Hebrew—*Ani huhani harishon af ani haaharon*, which means literally, 'An *I* which is an *I-He* is the first, and an *I* which is only an *I* is the last').

I saw prisoners who in prayer had not remained a simple 'I' but had become an 'I-He'. They so identified with the One to whom they prayed that it seemed as if the very touch of their garments healed.

The 'I' with its many petitions and problems, its thoughts, its hopes, its doubts and despair, had been consumed in the fire of God's love and had reached the supreme heights of his serenity. It was worth fourteen years of prison to witness one such prayer.

But those who arrived at such a plane of spiritual exaltation did not last long. Usually they died or were made to die, like Suciu, Ghica, Gafencu, Florea.

Did we have the experience of answered and rejected prayers? We knew the promise, 'Whatsoever ye shall ask in prayer, believing, ye shall receive' (Matthew 21:22). We discovered, quite simply, that we had misunderstood it. Only what we ask *in* prayer will be granted. Christians usually ask for what they had considered desirable *before starting to pray*. This, we learned, misses the point. When you understand the essence of real prayer, you forget even yourself, let alone the many demands you had before kneeling.

A prayer I often repeated was, 'Let him kiss me with the kisses of his mouth' (Song of Solomon 1:2). A bride can be sure she will receive whatever she asks of the bridegroom when they are in each other's embrace, when his ardent kisses have brought her to a paroxysm of love. For this only the sexual union provides an adequate image. The lover caresses the beloved in order to fulfill her ardent desire: the only thing she wishes at that moment.

What problems, one conjectures, would Juliet, a girl of fourteen, have brought to Romeo on their only bridal night? She must have had her difficulties. Possibly she missed her exams. Girls in love are not good at school. A talkative nurse angered her. But in the bridegroom's embrace, problems receive no solutions. They simply cease to exist.

My eight-year old granddaughter overheard discussions about problems in a meeting of our mission board. Later she asked me, 'Grandpa, where does the word "problem" occur in the Bible?' I had to answer truthfully, 'Nowhere'. 'Then,' she replied, 'why do you all look so worried about something that is not in the Bible?'

As long as you talk to God only about problems, your conversation does not yet deserve the name of believing prayer. You call him 'Almighty God', and so he is. But it is not fitting to bother the prime minister with matters a police officer could handle. As children we trouble him with little things, and he is gracious in his loving response. But now we can do so much better than bring him our small demands. Perhaps even God longs to be loved 'for love's sake only'.

In the exceptional circumstances of prison life, there were some prayers that were in a classification all their own.

One of the most terrible tortures in prison was the misery of erotic hallucinations. We suspected that our food contained drugs to exacerbate it. The young men were driven to madness. Young girls, secretaries of the prison staff, were paraded before them in miniskirts. Then months passed when no one ever saw a woman.

I knew one Christian who prayed at that time, 'God, give me more sexual obsessions. Give me the sexual obsessions of many who suffer from them in the free world. There they can wreak havoc and destroy lives. Here every naked girl I fantasize receives a prayer. I ask this, not because I would be better than those who fall in sin, but because I am in a cell.' I was told that such insistent prayer worked.

Female images continued to appear but with the aspect of

redeemed girls thankful for having been cared for and turned away from sin.

The air was very bad in prison. We were crowded together like rats in a cage—two hundred of us emaciated humans, sleeping on four tiers, fulfilling all our needs in the common bucket, eating together any way we could. We were in rags, unkempt, unwashed. Cells were sometimes heated in summer just for torture's sake. Many died of suffocation. Every breath, though noxious, was precious.

Even this was a blessing. It taught us the value of right breathing in prayer. There exists a breathing which imparts life and the Holy Spirit. God breathed the breath of life into Adam. Jesus breathed the Spirit on the apostles (John 20:22).

The sinner is like a wild ass that *snuffs* the wind (Jeremiah 2:24). Some *neigh* after their neighbour's wife (Jeremiah 5:8). Persecutors *breathe out threatenings and slaughter* (Acts 9:1).

Orthodox priests, imitating the act of Jesus, breathe three times on persons as part of the baptismal rite. Hence, it is not a matter of indifference how you breathe in prayer. Neither is it inconsequential how you speak or how you look. 'Thou hast ravished my heart with one of thine eyes,' says the Lord (Song of Solomon 4:9).

Whatever your words in prayer, God can read anger or lust in your breathing. I admired some saints in prison for their quiet, serene, rhythmic breathing, the breathing of men who had neither attachment for nor revulsion toward the world. They were simply unperturbed.

Once a prisoner had formed the habit of this serene breathing, as deep as possible without unusual effort, he retained the habit in grave danger, in times of severe beatings or torture, as well as in moments of ugly quarrels. I observed saints breathing in this holy manner, deeply, evenly. Fear, trembling, strife, even sin, I believe, become impossible if one breathes for a few minutes slowly, rhythmically, while saying a quiet prayer.

Recollection is always one-sided, even biased. No one recalls everything exactly as it happened. Pride keeps one from saying the whole truth. Selective repetition twists not only the facts but also the personality. One becomes retroactively what one wishes to have been.

I realise that I myself am in this danger. Desiring to tell the whole world about the beauty of the saints in chains, I may fail to reveal the darker side.

There were times of neglect or superficial prayer when imprisoned believers uttered prayers of rebellion against God in words that, taken in isolation, might almost be called blasphemous, as were many of the words of Job and David. 'Oh, that my grief were thoroughly weighed,' murmured Job, '...it would be heavier than the sands of the sea. Therefore my words are rash' (Job 6:2, in Hebrew).

Therese of Avila once prayed, 'Lord, if I saw one of your brothers in such danger, what would I not do to deliver him. Are you not at least as good as I?' And, 'O Lord, how true it is to say that as soon as one renders you a service, you pay him with a great tribulation.' But, she added, 'How precious is this recompense to those who have for you a true love if you understand its value' (*Therese of Avila*, by Pierre Lauzeral, Apostolat d'Editions, 1981).

In the Romanian prison of Piteshti, Christians were compelled over a period of two years to eat their faeces and drink urine, after these excreta had been 'consecrated' in a blasphemous mass. God heard at that time many ungracious words from his children. When some stronger man tried to remind others that we were God's chosen people, he could count on the reply, 'then let God choose someone else!' The hurt was too great.

Who had been hurt? The only entity which can be hurt is the *I*, which should long since have been denied. If we had died with Christ as we were intended to do, well, what does a corpse care about the food it gets?

The burnt offering of the self had not yet been consumed, it had not burned completely. Therefore we were angry. In commitment nothing remains but ashes. Ashes cannot revert back to firewood. Therefore Jesus speaks about repentance 'in ashes'.

When we had the grace to realise this, the serenity returned.

Today I live in the free world. In my world-wide travels on behalf of *The Christian Missions to the Communist World*, I encounter many difficulties of my own and am confronted with countless problems of others who are desperate for help. Sometimes I feel the burdens are too great, and long for the companionship of the saints in prison and for those moments of serene exaltation when heaven seemed very near. Other times I wonder that God can bear all the griefs and sorrows and complaints with which we burden him.

But as for me, I have learned in the deep furnace of affliction that God is my beloved, and that in his embrace I am ravished. Why he chose me and continues to love me, with all my failings, is not for me to say. For me it is sufficient to burn in the taper of his love.

'Though he slay me, yet will I trust him' (Job 13:15). Don't try to mend a broken heart. God loves it broken (Psalm 51). The atom releases energy only when it is split. The broken heart and its prayer *'in extremis'* has a tremendous force.